Vampires

A Very Peculiar History™

With added bite

'Welcome to my house!
Enter freely and of your own free will!'
Bram Stoker, Dracula (1897)

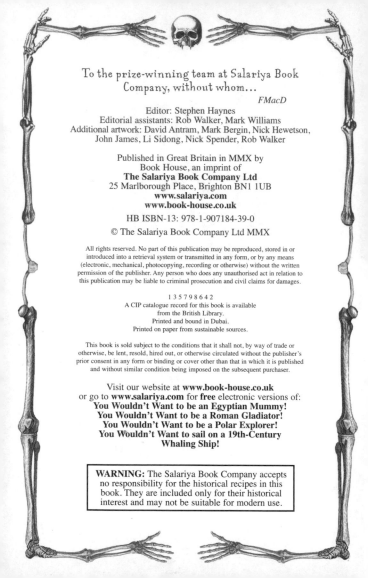

To the prize-winning team at Salariya Book
Company, without whom…

FMacD

Editor: Stephen Haynes
Editorial assistants: Rob Walker, Mark Williams
Additional artwork: David Antram, Mark Bergin, Nick Hewetson,
John James, Li Sidong, Nick Spender, Rob Walker

Published in Great Britain in MMX by
Book House, an imprint of
The Salariya Book Company Ltd
25 Marlborough Place, Brighton BN1 1UB
www.salariya.com
www.book-house.co.uk

HB ISBN-13: 978-1-907184-39-0

1 3 5 7 9 8 6 4 2
A CIP catalogue record for this book is available
from the British Library.
Printed and bound in Dubai.
Printed on paper from sustainable sources.

Visit our website at **www.book-house.co.uk**
or go to **www.salariya.com** for **free** electronic versions of:
You Wouldn't Want to be an Egyptian Mummy!
You Wouldn't Want to be a Roman Gladiator!
You Wouldn't Want to be a Polar Explorer!
**You Wouldn't Want to sail on a 19th-Century
Whaling Ship!**

WARNING: The Salariya Book Company accepts
no responsibility for the historical recipes in this
book. They are included only for their historical
interest and may not be suitable for modern use.

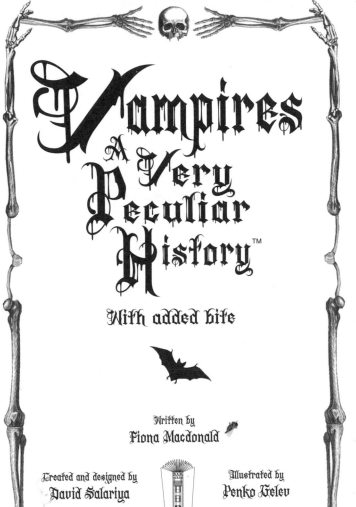

Vampires
A Very Peculiar History™

With added bite

Written by
Fiona Macdonald

Created and designed by
David Salariya

Illustrated by
Penko Gelev

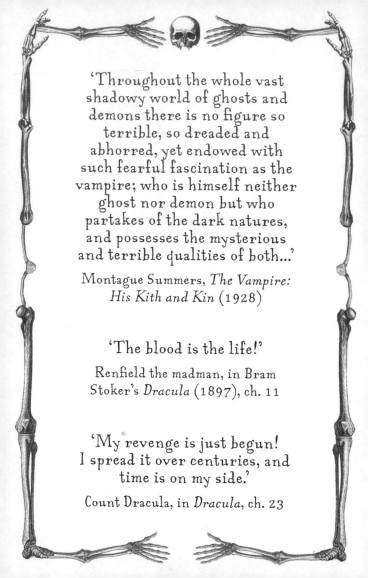

'Throughout the whole vast shadowy world of ghosts and demons there is no figure so terrible, so dreaded and abhorred, yet endowed with such fearful fascination as the vampire; who is himself neither ghost nor demon but who partakes of the dark natures, and possesses the mysterious and terrible qualities of both...'

Montague Summers, *The Vampire: His Kith and Kin* (1928)

'The blood is the life!'

Renfield the madman, in Bram Stoker's *Dracula* (1897), ch. 11

'My revenge is just begun! I spread it over centuries, and time is on my side.'

Count Dracula, in *Dracula*, ch. 23

Contents

Putting vampires†

Old-World vampires

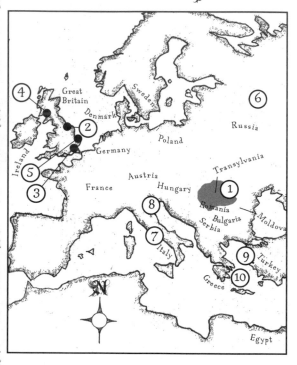

on the map

New-World witches

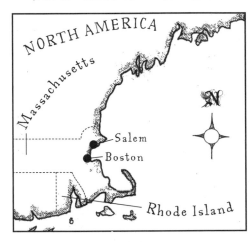

Places mentioned in the text

1. Bran Castle
2. Whitby
3. London
4. Glasgow
5. Norwich
6. Novgorod
7. Rome
8. Venice
9. Lesbos
10. Mykonos

Introduction

This book is not like most histories. It is not about great leaders, heroes and explorers, or ancient empires, lost civilisations, invasions, migrations and wars. Instead, it looks at the history of an idea. It tells how a completely imaginary creature – the vampire – came to be created.

Vampires do not exist – and they never have done. As living dead bodies, they contradict themselves. They are impossible! Even so, vampires have had extraordinary power over

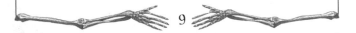

real living people, as well as over their film, TV and storybook victims. Vampire stories are thrilling – and fun. But they are not just entertainment. In the past, belief in vampires led to many deaths – of real men and women. Even today, a few people have tried to claim that 'being a vampire' allows them to kill or torture. Belief in vampires has been – and still can be – seriously bloody.

The first vampires

Today's vampire beliefs have developed over many thousands of years. They are a strange mixture of solemn religion and crazy superstitions, traditional folklore and the latest media fashions.

We do not know how old these beliefs are, but they appear in the earliest myths and legends from many parts of the world. And, very often, the spirit or life force in a body was symbolised by its blood. If that blood were taken away, the person it came from would die. But – so people thought – the blood might have the power to renew life in the person who had taken it!

Introduction

Here's a description, written over 100 years ago, of a classic vampire:

It is perfectly white – perfectly bloodless. The eyes look like polished tin; the lips are drawn back, and the principal feature next to those dreadful eyes is the teeth – the fearful-looking teeth – projecting like those of some wild animal, hideously, glaringly white, and fang-like. It approaches the bed with a strange, gliding movement. It clashes together the long nails that literally appear to hang from the finger ends...

He drags her head to the bed's edge. He forces it back by the long hair still entwined in his grasp. With a plunge he seizes her neck in his fang-like teeth – a gush of blood, and a hideous sucking noise follows. The girl has swooned,[1] and the vampyre is at his hideous repast![2]

from Varney the Vampire *(1847)*
James Malcolm Rymer

1. *swooned: fainted.*
2. *repast: meal.*

Powerful stuff! But where did this image of a bloodthirsty vampire come from? Vampires are not like cats or dogs – we don't see them around us. So how do we know what they look like, or how they behave? How and why were vampires invented? Read on, and find out more!

Eternal life

Death comes to us all, but, over the centuries, countless billions of people have wished that they, or their loved ones, might live for ever. They have often tried to preserve their honoured dead – for example, in ancient Egypt, by turning them into mummies, or, in early China, by burying them in suits of precious jade. They have left food and drink beside burials, hoping to nourish buried bodies, and regularly visited tombs, to talk to dead ancestors.

Some living people have also tried to think how the spirits of the dead might feel. In doing so, they have dreamed up imaginary beings,

such as ghosts, dybbuks[1] – and vampires. All these creatures have been unable to rest in their graves – and have longed for a new life after death. Some have also sought revenge for untimely or unlawful killings.

Many of these imagined 'living dead' have been timid, frail and invisible. But not vampires! They are violent and aggressive (even if this is disguised under a surface layer of charm), and have larger-than-life revolting, undecayed, bodies: twisted, blood-red (or deathly pale), bloated and grimacing.

Like ghosts, vampires haunt places where they once lived, appearing mysteriously, then vanishing. But, unlike ghosts, vampires are always hungry! In their eagerness to get food, they bite, suck, strangle and suffocate. They need meat or excrement (ugh!) or sex or (mostly) blood to survive. Once satisfied, they sleep in their graves – but only until their appetite comes back again…

---

1. In Jewish tradition, a dybbuk is the soul of a dead person which possesses a living person – often because it has unfinished business in the world of the living.

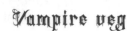

Vampire veg

Some past peoples have believed that the life-force of other living things besides humans might be dangerous. Some eastern Europeans were terrified by vampire fruits and vegetables. If stored in warm, damp conditions, pumpkins and watermelons can ooze a sticky red liquid – which superstitious farming families claimed was blood. They feared that, when hungry, the melon or pumpkin might try to attack them.

Looks can kill!

And, if vampire vegetables don't get you, here's a scary reminder. Just a glance from a *vrykolakas* – a traditional Greek country vampire – can kill!

It's time to look at blood, and why it's so nourishing. Come with me to Chapter 1!

Chapter One

Life Force
A very bloody business

We all need blood to live. That has been known since ancient times. Many people in the past also believed that blood shaped a person's character – for good or bad. In the first century AD, Roman writer Pliny the Elder reported that spectators rushed to drink the blood of dying gladiators, hoping that it would make them brave and strong. Later, around 1300, Petrus de Abano, professor of medicine at Padua University, warned that drinking lepers' blood would make you mad.

An average human body contains about 5 litres of blood. (Big men have a bit more, small women a little less.) Without blood, we would die. But what, precisely, is it? Where does it come from? And how does it keep us alive?

Floating cells

Blood is a mixture of microscopic living cells floating in a clear, yellowish liquid called *plasma*.

• **Red blood cells** (*erythrocytes*) carry oxygen (a gas essential for human tissues to function) around the body. The oxygen is carried by a protein in red cells called *haemoglobin*, which gives blood its deep red colour.

• **White blood cells** (*leukocytes*) fight infections and destroy old or damaged cells before they can harm the body.

• **Platelets** (*thrombocytes*) help the blood to clot and cover cuts and grazes. This prevents dangerous bacteria getting into the body. If blood did not clot, we might bleed to death from a tiny scratch.

• **Plasma** is about 90 per cent water, but also contains hormones (chemical messengers produced by glands), glucose (made by the liver, from food, to supply muscles with energy), carbon dioxide (a waste gas) and minute traces of many other substances. All of these are essential to keep the body working properly.

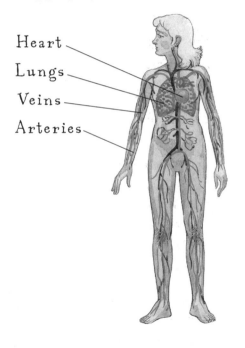

Heart

Lungs

Veins

Arteries

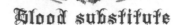

Blood substitute

According to legend, Medea, a queen – and witch! – in ancient Greece, used a magic mixture to make a sick old man young and strong again.

First, she mixed the following ingredients in a big bronze cauldron:

- Plant roots
- Herb juices
- Rare pebbles
- Sparkling frost (collected at full moon, of course!)
- The wings of an owl
- The guts of a werewolf
- The flesh of a snake
- The liver of a stag
- And the head of a 900-year-old crow!

Then Medea cut the old man's throat and let all the old blood drain away, before making him drink her magic mixture. It is claimed that, straight away, his white hair turned black and his thin, feeble body became fit and healthy again.

Even if you can get hold of the ingredients, do not, not, not try this at home. It will kill you!

18

Round and round

Blood is circulated (pumped around the body) by the heart, a collection of very powerful muscles, which keeps beating non-stop, day and night, for as long as you live. To feel the beat, place your hand in the middle of your chest, slightly to the left. Your heart is there, safely inside a bony cage – your ribs!

The circulation of blood was demonstrated in experiments by English doctor William Harvey in 1628 – though Muslim scholars such as Avicenna knew quite a lot about circulation and heart function even in the Middle Ages.

The heart works closely with the lungs to keep the human body alive. It pushes blood through two separate circuits – networks of tiny tubes, called arteries and veins. Arteries carry blood full of oxygen from the lungs to the rest of the body. Once the oxygen has been used, veins carry the stale blood back to the lungs. There, its red blood cells are 'refilled' with oxygen, ready to be pumped through the arteries again.

Bloody marvellous!

- About 8 per cent of our body weight is blood.

- Blood in the arteries, which contains oxygen, is bright scarlet; blood in the veins, where the oxygen has been used up, is dark crimson.

- If human bodies are starved of oxygen for longer than about 4 minutes, they will die.

- All human blood is red, but some sea creatures have blood that is blue, orange or green.

- Red blood cells live for only 120 days. New ones are being made all the time.

- Red and white blood cells are produced by the marrow (soft core) of large bones; platelets are made in the liver.

- In the past, people thought that blood supply influenced character. A man with plenty of blood would be 'sanguine':[1] brave, cheerful, energetic and hot-tempered.

- When it's cold outside, blood flows back towards the centre of the body to keep it warm. That's why our fingers and toes go white in frosty weather.

- Exercise, and strong feelings – such as fear of vampires! – make the heart pump harder and the blood flow faster.

1. *From* sanguis, *the Latin for 'blood'.*

Go for the throat!

Where's the best place for a vampire to bite a human victim? Take my advice, and go for the throat. It's traditional, but there are also good scientific reasons:

- Big arteries run on either side of the neck, taking blood from the heart and lungs to the brain.

- The blood these arteries carry is filled with oxygen. It will be fresher and contain fewer waste products than stale blood from veins.

- Necks are thin and scrawny. The arteries there are not buried deep in fat, but lie close under the skin.

Easy see, easy bite – that's my motto!

- Arterial blood is at higher pressure than blood in veins. It spurts and splashes, so you're sure of a fast flow. Ideal for a hasty meal!

Other vampire friends tell me that they prefer to bite and suck elsewhere. They choose the chest or the stomach. There are very big arteries there. But this method is not so good if your chosen victim is stout. You'll soon find that layers of fat will get in the way!

Rabbit starvation

Even if Dracula and his fellow vampires had been able to get enough blood to satisfy their hunger, they would not have been well nourished. Blood contains a fair amount of protein, but not enough fat or carbohydrate (starch) and fibre to provide a balanced diet.

Very probably, Dracula and other vampires would have suffered from 'rabbit starvation' – a condition which gets its name from Native American people who were forced by bad weather to survive by eating the lean meat of rabbits for weeks on end, with no other nourishment.

Sufferers from rabbit starvation reported that they soon developed terrible diarrhoea, and felt weak and tired all the time. Their bodies simply could not digest all the lean meat they were consuming without fats and carbohydrates to balance it. Although eating food, they were starving!

I'm not good for you! Honest!

Whooosh!

Bloodstained clues

Since the early 20th century, forensic scientists have collected minute traces of blood and other body fluids from crime scenes and victims' bodies. By matching these to blood samples taken from suspects, they have been able to solve many crimes. Disturbingly, forensic blood analysis has also suggested that some famous criminals – including the notorious Dr Crippen, executed in 1910 for the bloody murder of his wife – were NOT guilty!

Blood as medicine

Ancient Greek doctor Galen believed that the blood of a dog or a weasel could cure dangerous rabies. The ancient Romans had a saying: 'Your own blood rubbed on a wound will ease the pain.' In the Arctic, Dark Age hunters drank seal blood as a cure for scurvy.[1]

From around 1600 to 1800 doctors and scientists in many European lands began to experiment with blood transfusions. Always these were from animals to animals, or from animals to people. Mostly they failed – partly because it was not yet understood that different blood groups must not be mixed.

1. This may actually have worked – but the other 'cures' mentioned here certainly can't have done.

What's in a name?

Because blood is vital for life, it has also been used as a name for many other important things, such as family, energy – and violence.

- **Blue blood** Noble ancestry. It used to be said that royal or noble blood was 'blue', to distinguish it from ordinary people's red blood. (Veins often look blue when seen through fair skin, and in earlier centuries fair skin was fashionable.)

- **Get one's blood up** Become angry.

- **Baptism of blood** Martyrdom.

- **Blood brothers** Very close friends, linked by a ceremony in which blood was mixed and shared. **NEVER, EVER DO THIS! BLOOD CARRIES KILLER DISEASES THAT CANNOT BE CURED.**

- **Blood-and-thunder** Extremely dramatic and violent.

- **Blood horse** A thoroughbred (well-bred) racehorse.

- **Blood is thicker than water** Family links are stronger than anything else.

- **Blood libel** Blaming a whole tribe or ethnic group for a crime or problem.

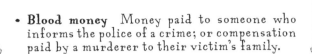

- **Blood money** Money paid to someone who informs the police of a crime; or compensation paid by a murderer to their victim's family.

- **Have blood on one's hands** Be guilty.

- **In cold blood** Calmly, deliberately, without passion.

- **Make one's blood boil** Make one very angry indeed.

- **Make one's blood run cold** Fill one with fear and horror.

- **Young blood** A daring young man.

Last but not least:

- **Bloodbath** Normally, this is another word for 'massacre' or 'mass killing'. But – according to rumour – the pharaohs of Ancient Egypt took the word at face value. They took baths in big buckets of fresh blood, believing this would help them live for ever.

- **Bad blood** In the past, people thought that blood could cause diseases. They 'let blood' (cut a vein so that 'bad' blood ran out) to try to get rid of an illness. Or else they used leeches – blood-sucking parasites, like huge fat worms – to drain blood away.

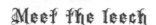

Meet the leech

As a blood-sucker myself, I have to admire leeches. Here are some leech facts and figures:

- A leech is like a long tube divided into 34 segments.

- It can grow to 20 cm long, or more.

- It has a powerful sucker – which clings to skin – at each end.

- To drink, a leech bores a hole in the skin, then spits a substance to stop blood clotting.

- Leeches feed for 2 to 3 hours. They are attached to the skin all that time.

- They can suck up to 10 times their own weight in blood.

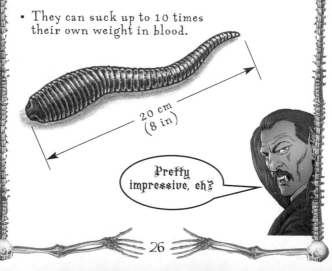

20 cm
(8 in)

Pretty impressive, eh?

Inspired by science?

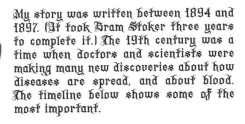

My story was written between 1894 and 1897. (It took Bram Stoker three years to complete it.) The 19th century was a time when doctors and scientists were making many new discoveries about how diseases are spread, and about blood. The timeline below shows some of the most important.

By the 1890s, there had also been a few successful experiments with blood transfusion. In Bram Stoker's book, blood from four strong, brave, healthy men is used to save the life of one of my favourite victims, Lucy Westenra – for a while.

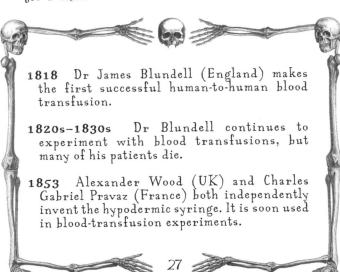

1818 Dr James Blundell (England) makes the first successful human-to-human blood transfusion.

1820s–1830s Dr Blundell continues to experiment with blood transfusions, but many of his patients die.

1853 Alexander Wood (UK) and Charles Gabriel Pravaz (France) both independently invent the hypodermic syringe. It is soon used in blood-transfusion experiments.

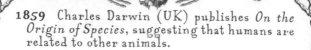

1859 Charles Darwin (UK) publishes *On the Origin of Species*, suggesting that humans are related to other animals.

1862 Louis Pasteur (France) discovers bacteria – invisibly small living organisms that can spread from one person to another and cause disease.

1865 Gregor Mendel (Moravia – now part of the Czech Republic) discovers the laws of heredity.

1870s–1880s Sir William Osler (Canada) and Giulio Bizzozero (Italy) explain how blood clotting works.

1885 Louis Pasteur (France) invents vaccine against rabies – a deadly disease passed on by bites from infected people or animals.

1900 Karl Landsteiner (Austria) discovers blood groups (varieties of blood that cannot be mixed). This helps doctors work out how to give safer blood transfusions.

1901 Ilya Mechnikov (Russia; also known as Elie Metchnikoff) discovers how white blood cells fight infection.

Chapter Two

Restless souls

Vampire myths and superstitions

Ghosts and blood-suckers have a long history. For many centuries, they've appeared with different names, and in many strange shapes and sizes. But here's a surprise! Compared with those oldies, classic vampires like Dracula are just newcomers. They sprang to ghastly life – complete with fangs – some time around AD 1600. How were they created?

The idea and image of a classic, Dracula-like vampire came from two very different sources: traditional, pagan blood-sucker myths and early Christian traditions. The myths told of dangerous ghosts, and how dead humans might turn into evil, godless monsters. Christian priests taught that sinful people (and, sometimes, their victims) could never rest in peace. When these two traditions were mixed together, the classic vampire was born.

Is death the end of existence? If not, what happens to people who have passed away? Do they all rest in peace – or are some doomed to linger: troubled, restless, unquiet... **undead?**

The dead are dangerous!

This ballad (traditional song) was first sung in England around AD 1400. It is based on a pagan (pre-Christian) belief: that the dead somehow go on living, and are dangerous. Similar ideas are found in songs and stories from all over Europe.

This ballad also highlights another feature belonging to later, classic vampires. Although dead and ghastly, they can be irresistibly attractive. People want to kiss them!

'The wind doth blow today, my love,
And a few small drops of rain;
I never had but one true love,
In cold grave she was lain.

'I'll do as much for my true love
As any young man may;
I'll sit and mourn all at her grave
For a twelvemonth and a day.'

The twelvemonth and a day being up,
The dead began to speak:
'Oh who sits weeping on my grave,
And will not let me sleep?'

''Tis I, my love, sits on your grave,
And will not let you sleep;
For I crave one kiss of your clay-cold lips,
And that is all I seek.'

'You crave one kiss of my clay-cold lips;
But my breath smells earthy strong;
If you have one kiss of my clay-cold lips,
Your time will not be long.'

Asvid and Asmund

Not all the dead were loving. This pagan Viking story was first recorded by Saxo Grammaticus, a Danish writer who lived around AD 1200. Here it is retold:

Asvid

Asmund

Warriors Asvid and Asmund were comrades, bold, brave and loyal. They always fought side by side, and vowed that not even death would part them. But Asvid was killed, and buried in the Viking way, with his horse and his dog, under a tall cairn (heap of stones). True to his promise, and with amazing courage, Asmund volunteered to be buried – alive! – alongside him.

Shortly afterwards, King Erik of Sweden rode past the cairn. 'Aha!', he thought, 'a fine new warrior's tomb! I bet there's gold and silver inside. A brave man is always buried with his favourite things – his sword, his helmet and his jewellery.'

Greedily, King Erik decided to break open the cairn and steal the dead warrior's treasure. His men rolled away the cairn-stones, smashed a hole in the wooden burial chamber, and tied a rope round the king's youngest, smallest servant. 'Grab any gold you can see!', they told him, as they lowered him into the grave. 'Then – don't worry! – we'll haul you back to the surface again.'

They waited, and soon the rope twitched, once, twice, three times. 'Heave away! That's our signal!' they cried. But the load was surprisingly heavy. 'What mighty treasures must be here!' they gasped. 'What a golden prize for King Erik!'

It was not gold. No! It was a haggard, bloodstained man, alive, but gasping and trembling. It was Asmund! And he had a terrifying story to tell…

Each night, after dark, his dead comrade Asvid came back to life, and was always ravenously hungry. First he ate his horse, then he ate his dog – and then he turned upon Asmund. With cruel, long, sharp nails, he gouged great chunks from Asmund's face, and ripped off his ear.

Was Asmund fated to be eaten, bit by bit, every night, by his dead friend and comrade? No! With a desperate effort, he drove a wooden stake through Asvid's heart – and killed him, for ever.

Vile bodies – or holy ones?

At the same time as these ancient ballads and stories were being enjoyed, the Christian Church was telling people throughout Europe to think about the dead in a very different fashion.

The Church taught that Jesus Christ had risen from the dead and ascended into heaven. At some future time, he would return to earth, to judge the living – and the dead. When that happened, Christian believers should hope to rise again from their graves to meet their maker face to face.

Exactly how dead bodies might rise was a holy mystery, accepted by faithful believers. But in practical terms, the early Church also understood that buried human bodies decayed. Its holy books and rituals contained words that recognised this fact, such as 'Dust [earth] thou art, and to dust thou wilt return.' And many Christians held special services at gravesides 40 days after a body had been buried. By that time, a corpse would normally be well decayed, so a dead person's soul could leave it and begin the journey towards heaven – or hell.

That, at least, was what everyone expected to happen to a normal buried body. But there were exceptions. It was said that saints' bodies remained 'uncorrupted' in the tomb. Their wholesome condition after death reflected the saints' holy lifestyles. Cathedrals and monasteries collected relics of well-preserved saintly bodies; pilgrims flocked to kneel and pray beside them.

Perfect – and perfectly preserved

St Isidore 'the Farmer', a poor Spanish peasant, lived a blameless life of hard work and poverty. He was famously kind to his neighbours, and to farm animals. The only time he got into trouble – he arrived late for work after going to church to pray – a white-robed angel appeared to do his ploughing for him and calm his master's anger.

Isidore died in AD 1130, and was buried, like most peasants, in a simple hole in the ground. But 40 years later, his corpse was dug up again. (It was said that instructions to do this were received in a dream.) To everyone's surprise, Isidore's body 'looked as if it had only just died'. Soon, people said that praying to him worked miracles. He became a saint.

In 1662, Isidore's body was dug up again, with important people as witnesses. Again, it seemed freshly buried, and, amazingly, was said to give off 'a heavenly odour'.

Less happily, the Church also taught that there was another reason why certain people's bodies might not decay. They might not have been buried with proper Christian ceremonies, or they might have been refused burial in holy ground. (That was the fate of suicides, who were buried at lonely crossroads – and were believed to haunt them!)

Rich, powerful people sometimes died far from home. They wanted to be buried in their local church, but there was no way of getting their bodies there before they rotted completely. So expert 'packers' ripped the inner organs out, stripped the flesh away, and pickled it, with the bones, in vinegar. Church leaders were absolutely horrified.

A few sinners were so bad that they became 'beastly': no longer human! The normal rules of change and decay did not apply to them. If their well-preserved bodies ever happened to be discovered, their unnatural condition only proved what monsters they had become.

[If a man] offends the Lord his God by a proud and disobedient use of his free will, he shall become subject to death, and live as the beasts do, the slave of appetite, and doomed to eternal punishment.

St Augustine, c.AD 420

Now let me take you back in time!

Imagine that you're a poor, uneducated villager living in wild countryside somewhere in Europe any time between around AD 1000 and 1600. Your life is nasty, dirty and short. As a child, your grandparents filled your mind with stories of monsters and magic. Now, you go to church and listen to priests; you believe that, without Christian rituals to protect you from the cradle to the grave, your soul will be in deadly danger.

You know nothing about science – after all, many scientific discoveries have not yet been made. You see shocking, upsetting things: your friends die young; your crops wither in the fields. You are frightened by thunder and lightning; you fear hunger, cold and disease. You can't explain a lot of what happens in your life, and so you blame evil 'outsiders'. Perhaps these are strangers or foreigners; perhaps they're badly behaved neighbours. Or perhaps they are ghosts, devils – and vampires!

An English vampire

The following report was recorded by William of Newburgh, an English monk, around AD 1190:

A suspicious man was spying on his wife when he fell from his hiding place and was badly injured. His friends urged him to ask God to forgive all his sins (this would save his soul), but he was far too angry. That night, he died.

His friends got a priest to bury him, but the dead man could not rest in his grave. Every night, his monstrous spirit wandered through the village, trailed by hell-hounds howling furiously. Everyone barred their doors and dared not go outside, for fear of being attacked. Even so, they could not escape the dead man's evil influence. The air all around was poisoned by the stench of his corpse; its 'pestiferous[1] breath' found its way into every house, spreading deadly disease…

What could the villagers do? Many fell ill and died; others ran away. Only two young men decided to take action: 'This evil spirit has

1. pestiferous: disease-carrying.

killed our father and many of our neighbours,' they said. 'Let us destroy it before it does more harm.'

They hurried to the graveyard, and began to dig. Soon they uncovered the corpse. It was swollen to an immense size, with a bloated face, all congested with blood. Its shroud[1] was torn to shreds…

In classic vampire stories, a torn shroud is a sign that the corpse is **not dead**. Instead, it has grown fangs and has been chewing...

The young men were not afraid. They thwacked the corpse with their spade – but out flowed 'an unstoppable stream of blood'. It was as if a monstrous leech (see page 26) had filled itself 'with the blood of many persons'.

Want to know what happened next? Turn to page 52!

1. shroud: the cloth in which a dead body is wrapped.

Seeing is believing!

Why did early vampire stories like this become so popular and so powerful? Probably because they served a very useful purpose. Believing in vampires helped explain strange events, from sudden death to odd night-time noises. They also helped people manage everyday worries by turning them into a named 'creature', with predictable – although horrid! – habits.

Vampires often appeared at times of religious dispute or political upheaval. They reflected conflicts and tensions in people's minds. And, when everything seemed to be going badly for a family or a community, a vampire attack was a useful way of blaming 'someone' for causing problems without accusing other villagers. Poor people needed to stay friends with their neighbours, just to survive!

The image of a vampire, with fangs and claws and/or swollen with blood, also helped people cope with the unpleasant, disturbing sight of a long-dead or badly injured body. A vampire corpse was subhuman; a good, ordinary person would not end up looking that way. However, vampire descriptions were not fantasies. People claimed to know what vampires looked like because they thought they'd seen one!

Take another time-travel trip!

Imagine, once again, that you are a poor villager. Someone you know has died (from disease, or an accident, or in childbirth or war). The priest has said prayers over their body. Now the corpse needs to be buried, so you go to the graveyard where strong men are digging a hole for it to lie in. The churchyard is small, and it's getting full. As they dig, they disturb a body that was buried there earlier.

But what's this? Aaargghh! The body's been transformed! It's no longer – for example – that strange old woman (was she a witch?), or that mean, cruel farmer. It's not even the pretty girl who was attacked, or the red-headed twin, or the seventh son of a seventh son, or the mysterious stranger, or anyone 'unusual'. No! the body's no longer human at all! It's turned into a vampire!

What's really happened?

It's larger than life, and blood-red!

It's swollen by gases and beginning to rot.

Its stomach looks full – has it eaten?

More gases, plus fluids from decomposing flesh!

It has fangs, it's grown a beard! Its nails have turned into claws!

Its gums have shrunk, so its teeth look longer. Its skin and muscles have tightened, so more hair and fingernails are on show.

Mystery man – or monster?

In AD 1047, a Russian chronicler wrote down the name of a man he called Upir Likhiy. The name means something like 'horrible vampire' – and it probably described a hated enemy of Prince Vladimir of Novgorod. This is the first recorded use of a word like 'vampire' in Europe. It's probably an insult; Vladimir's enemy was not a real-life blood-sucker... Or was he?

Are you sure she's dead?

Well, she doesn't look very well...

LE MERCVRE GALANT.

The publick memorialls of the years 1693 and 1694 speak of *oupires*, *vampires* or *ghosts* which are seen in *Poland* and above all *Russia*. They make their appearance from noon to midnight, & come to suck the blood of living men and animals in such abundance as that it sometimes flows from them at the nose, & principally at the ears, and sometimes the corpse *swims in its own blood* oozed out in its coffin.

This reviving being, or *oupire*, comes out of the grave & goes by night to *embrace and hug violently* his near relations and friends, and sucks their blood so much as to weaken or attenuate them, and at last cause their death. This persecution does not stop at a single person; it extends to the last person of the family, if the course be not interrupted by *cutting off the head* or *opening the heart* of the ghost, whose corpse is found in his coffin, *yielding, flexible, swollen, and rubicund*, although he may have been dead some time.

There proceeeds from his body *a great quantity of blood*, which some mix up with flour to make *bread* of; & that bread when eaten protects them from being tormented by the spirit which returns no more.

M. DC. XCIV.
AVEC PRIVILEGE DV ROY.

Chapter Three

Haunted lands
Home of vampires

The report opposite comes from one of the first French newspapers. The writer, who prides himself on his education and his civilised manners, is clearly shocked – but enjoys telling the story. You'll recognise some of the bloodstained details from earlier vampire songs and legends – but, readers take note! – this is not fiction, but a *real-life* news report.

So it's official! You can read it in the papers! We classic vampires have been recognised as a public pest problem! Descriptions of our hauntings pour in from all over southern and eastern Europe; we've been found among Christian, Jewish and Muslim communities.

As you see, we east European vampires are not too fussy about whose blood we consume. We prefer to keep vampire activities within the family, if we can, but if supplies run short, we'll bite anybody!

I do hope you enjoyed the bit about the vampire bread. Perhaps you'd like the recipe some time?

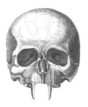

𝔇𝔬𝔫'𝔱 𝔭𝔞𝔫𝔦𝔠!

Belief in vampires was probably (just) better than being haunted by unnamed terrors, or trembling as bloodthirsty invaders marched into your homeland. Between around 1400 and 1800, eastern Europe saw many wars, conquests and invasions. Fighting led to chaos and lawlessness; bandits and warlords attacked each other, as well as armies sent by kings and queens. Old communities were disrupted; families became refugees. New arrivals spoke strange languages and lived in unfamiliar ways. There were also quarrels between Protestant, Roman Catholic and Orthodox Christians, and between Christians and Muslims. Perhaps it's no surprise that belief in vampires grew faster in this region than anywhere else.

However, thinking that a vampire was lurking round the corner – or waiting to rise from the local graveyard – was still pretty terrifying. From time to time, whole communities were gripped by 'vampire panic'. Normal, sane men and women listened to strange, supernatural rumours. They genuinely believed that a real, flesh-and-blood monster was close by. The most famous vampire panics took place in Hungary, Serbia and Wallachia (which now forms parts of Romania and Moldova) in the 1720s. But there were many more. All too often, they were fatal...

The sad case of Stanoska

A girl named Stanoska, who went to bed in perfect health, awoke in the night all in a tremble, shrieking dreadfully, saying that the son of Heyducq[1] Millo, who had been dead for nine weeks, had nearly strangled her in her sleep. From that moment she fell into a languishing state, and at the end of three days she died.

Report by monk and student of vampires, Dom Augustin Calmet, 1751 (see below, page 59)

The peculiar case of Peter Plogojowitz

In 1725, in Serbia, Peter died, aged 62. A poor farm worker, he is said to have returned from the dead to ask his son for food. His son refused, and died the next day. An 18th-century writer continues the story:

Two days later several individuals in the place fell ill, and in eight days nine of them were dead. Every one of these declared that Peter Plogojowitz was the sole cause of their illness. He had visited them in the night, thrown himself upon them, and sucked their blood.

1. *Heyducq: local commander.*

50

The awful case of Arnod Paole

From the same 18th-century observer:

Arnod Paole fell from a hay wagon and broke his neck. Arnod had in his lifetime often related how he had been tormented by a vampire.

Some twenty or thirty days after his death, several individuals complained that Arnod Paole had visited them, and four of these died. Accordingly, forty days after his burial he was exhumed, and found quite fresh and with blood running out of his eyes, ears and nostrils. His shirt and shroud were soaked with blood. The old skin and nails had fallen off and fresh ones had grown.

The body was at once burnt. But the mischief was not at an end, for everyone who has been bitten by a vampire becomes a vampire as well; and the trouble had become so great that orders were sent by Government to open all the graves of those who were supposed to have been vampire-bitten, report on their condition, and, if necessary, burn the bodies.

The investigators dug up and examined thirteen dead bodies, all from the same village graveyard. They found that ten were 'in vampire condition'; that is, fresh and plump, filled with blood, and with shocking, newly grown fangs or talons...

51

Direct action

Sufferers from 'vampire panic' huddled together in streets or churchyards, or refused to set foot out of doors. They shrieked, wept, trembled and prayed. They asked priests to hold special exorcism ceremonies to drive evil spirits away from their homes and farms. (Some priests were accused of encouraging the panic so they could profit from exorcism fees.) Sometimes, they used magic to 'explore' places where the dead were buried. That way, they hoped to detect future vampires before they became troublesome. But, most often, they took action themselves to try to destroy the vampire!

Remember the story on page 40 about the dead man (an early vampire) who brought disease to his community? Well, this is what happened to him:

The young men hauled his corpse up out of its grave, dragged it away from their village, laid it on a huge bonfire, hacked it open, took out its heart, tore that into pieces, lit the bonfire and scattered the pieces on the flames! The vampire never troubled the villagers again.

Suspect a looming vampire attack?

Prevention is better than cure. Try this magic method:

Send a pure young boy on a fine black horse to ride over all the graves in a churchyard. If the horse refuses to step on any grave, then you'll know the person buried there is turning into a vampire!

Digging up a suspect corpse then burning it was one way of destroying a vampire, but east European villagers also tried many others:

- Hammering a pointed wooden stake right through the vampire's heart. Aspen (poplar) wood was believed to be the best, for religious reasons – old stories told how the cross on which Jesus died was made of aspen. Maple, hawthorn or whitethorn were also excellent.

- Stabbing through the heart with a long, sharp dagger that had been sprinkled with holy water.

- Cutting off a vampire's head (at a single blow – otherwise it would come back to life), then placing the head between its knees.

- Cooking the body in boiling oil before burning it on a bonfire.

- Shooting the vampire's body with a silver bullet that had been blessed by a priest.

- Burying the vampire on an island. Vampires could not – by themselves – travel across salt water.

- Eating vampire blood – if you could face it!

The Vampire of Venice

In 2006, Italian archaeologists uncovered the remains of a female 'vampire' (opposite). The woman, aged about 60, had died of plague in 1576, and been buried in a mass grave on an island near Venice. When more plague victims died, the grave had been opened to bury them, and her body had been discovered with a tattered shroud, swollen limbs, and gaping mouth. All these had been caused by natural decay (as Dracula explains on pages 43–44), but 16th-century people did not understand this. So they forced a brick between the dead woman's jaws to stop her eating flesh – or anything else – and drinking blood. It is still there today.

They shouldn't treat a respectable woman like this. It really sticks in my throat.

The story of the Venetian 'vampire' is true, but still takes a lot of swallowing.

Vampire ancestors

Bloody beauty

The ancient Greek Gorgon was beautiful – but deadly. (*Gorgos* means 'terrible'.) She had sharp fangs and waving snakes for hair. A single glance from her flashing eyes turned men to stone. And half her blood – drawn from her left-hand side – was a fast-acting, fatal poison.

But the terrible Gorgon also had mighty protective powers. Ancient Greek people put pictures of her lovely face on their weapons, coins, houses – and tombstones – to guard against enemies. And blood from the Gorgon's right-hand side was so strong that – so they said – it could bring men back to life again.

Hungry ghosts

Vegetarian vampires? Possibly not, but this ancient Roman tradition may have helped inspire some later vampire stories. The Romans feared *lemures* – the evil, greedy spirits of the dead. Lemures were said to visit Roman houses at the festival of Lemuria– three dangerous days in May (9th, 11th, 13th). Their aim? To carry off the living. Wishing to protect his family, the head of each household scattered black beans at doorways. He hoped that the lemures would take the beans, instead of human victims. Black beans were thought to be sinisterly powerful and ritually unclean; priests were forbidden to touch them.

> Wait! There are some people you've forgotten: the Bulgarian Vampire Bottlers![1]

COMING TO YOUR VILLAGE
FOR ONE WEEK ONLY
☞ BULGARIA'S FINEST ☜
VAMPIRE BOTTLERS

* Trained and experienced team *
* We destroy troublesome vampires
in SIX easy stages *
* Satisfaction guaranteed *

1. We arm ourselves with holy pictures of saints.

2. We lie in wait until a vampire passes.

3. Our holy pictures force the vampire to run until he has nowhere left to hide.

4. He has to seek shelter in our bottle – we put food inside it first, to tempt him.

5. We seal the bottle with a scrap of holy picture. That way, he can't escape.

6. Then we throw the bottle onto a good hot fire!

☞ DON'T DELAY! ☜
BOOK OUR EXPERT SERVICES NOW!!

1. *Readers – this is true! In Bulgaria, people made careers by claiming to catch vampires this way.*

57

Playing safe

On the Greek island of Lesbos, archaeologists have discovered the skeleton of a suspected vampire. A Muslim, he was buried in a secure stone chamber around AD 1800. How do they know he was a suspect? His neck, pelvis and ankle had all been nailed to the tomb with strong iron spikes about 20 cm long. Traditionally, this was yet another way of making sure that potential vampires could not rise from the dead to haunt the living.

'Barbarism and ignorance'

Vampire crazes happened in remote country districts, far from any centres of political power. But, if they got out of hand, they might prove a threat to law and order. Believing in vampires also seemed 'backward' and superstitious, at a time when the most powerful people in Europe prided themselves on their civilised, well-balanced and rational ideas. For all these reasons, European leaders, of Church and state, thought that they should be discouraged.

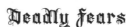

Deadly Fears

Dom Augustin Calmet (1692–1757) was a French Benedictine monk and scholar. He studied ancient holy texts and popular superstitions. In 1746 he published his *Dissertations sur les apparitions des anges, des démons et des esprits, et sur les revenants et vampires de Hongrie, de Bohème, de Moravie, et de Silésie.*[1] To Calmet's surprise, it became a best-seller – and provided inspiration for many poets and novelists (see Chapter 4).

Calmet did not believe in vampires. He explained outbreaks of vampire panic as mass hysteria (he called it 'epidemical fanaticism'). He suggested that the victims of 'pretended' vampires were killed by their own powerful fears, and not by any supernatural creatures.

It's lucky I'm not afraid of long words...

1. *Essays on Apparitions of Angels, Demons and Spirits, and on the Ghosts and Vampires of Hungary, Bohemia, Moravia and Silesia.*

Unbelievers

In 1755, Empress Maria Theresa of Austria, who ruled many kingdoms in central and eastern Europe, sent her personal doctor, Dutch-born Gerard van Swieten, to investigate the vampire craze. Other vampire hunters soon followed him.

Van Swieten was one of the top scientists of his time. He was calm and calculating; his knowledge was based on careful observations and reliable evidence. He suggested scientific explanations (such as the temperature of the graves, or unusual soil conditions) for all the supposed vampire burials. And he reported that the panics were caused only by 'superstitious willingness to believe, morbid and excitable imaginations, plus ignorance and naivety among the people.'

Other scientists agreed with him, and suggested extra reasons for outbreaks of vampire hysteria:

- Perhaps sick people – maybe in a coma, or with a serious mental illness – had mistakenly been buried while they were still alive.

- Sudden 'clusters' of deaths might have been caused by outbreaks of smallpox and plague. Both diseases were widespread in eastern Europe at this time.

- There had also been outbreaks of rabies, another killer disease, in 18th-century Europe. Victims 'ran wild' and often bit other humans.

- Perhaps wild animals – or tomb-robbers, or even floods or earth tremors – had opened up shallow graves. The dead had not risen by themselves!

Convinced by van Swieten's report, Maria Theresa banned all traditional vampire-killing customs – including beheading and burning – throughout her empire. Vampire panics, and belief in vampires, must be abolished!

But we vampires never die! Turn to Chapter 4 and find out how we soon became the latest literary fashion.

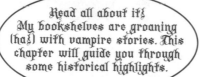

> Read all about it!
> My bookshelves are groaning
> (ha!) with vampire stories. This
> chapter will guide you through
> some historical highlights.

Brought to book

According to the *Oxford English Dictionary*,
the first known use of the word *vampire* in
print in England was in 1734. Then, a vampire
was described as 'a ghost who leaves his grave at
night and sucks the blood from the living'.

Chapter Four

Sensation seekers

The first vampire stories

The years from 1700 to 1900 saw a vast increase in the number of texts written about vampires. Descriptions of bloody vampire attacks and grisly vampire hunting were no longer hidden in dusty books written by and for religious scholars, or passed on only by word of mouth in communities where people could not read or write. Now, for the first time, as more and more vampire books appeared in print, a wider audience could enjoy the thrill of reading about frightful, fantastic vampires and sighing over the sufferings of their victims.

𝔗𝔯𝔞𝔳𝔢𝔩𝔩𝔢𝔯𝔰' 𝔱𝔞𝔩𝔢𝔰

The first descriptions of vampire attacks were presented as fact, not fiction. Mostly, they appeared in travellers' tales composed by wealthy young men who had spent a year travelling to complete their education. These vampire stories contrasted the 'primitive' folk beliefs of south and east Europe with the 'civilised' north and west. That made them all the more dangerous and exciting.

1741

This eyewitness account of a Greek vampire was written in 1718. It was translated into English almost 30 years later.

We were present at a very different Scene, and one very barbarous . . . which happened upon occasion of one of those Corpses, which they fancy come to life again after their interment.[1] The Man whose Story we are going to relate, was a Peasant of Mycone,[2] naturally ill-natur'd and quarrelsom; this is a Circumstance

1. interment: burial.   2. Mycone: Mykonos, a Greek island.

to be taken notice of in such cases: he was murder'd in the fields, no body knew how, or by whom. Two days after his being bury'd in a Chapel in the Town it was nois'd about[1] that he was seen to walk in the night with great haste, that he tumbled about Peoples Goods, put out their Lamps, griped them behind and a thousand other monky Tricks. . . .

On the tenth day they said one Mass in the Chapel where the Body was laid, in order to drive out the Demon which they imagin'd was got into it. After Mass, they took up the Body, and got every thing ready for pulling out its Heart . . .

. . . the Corpse stunk so abominably, that they were obliged to burn Frankincense; but this smoke mixing with the Exhalations[2] from the Carcass, increas'd the Stink, and began to muddle the poor Peoples Pericranies.[3] Their Imagination, struck with the Spectacle before them, grew full of Visions. . . .

from A Voyage into the Levant *[Middle East]*
Joseph Pitton de Tournefort (France)

1. *nois'd about: reported.*   2. *Exhalations: fumes, smells.*
3. *Pericranies: brains.*

Romantic revolution

By the late 1700s, many painters, musicians, philosophers and writers believed that 'civilised' western Europe had grown dull, backward-looking and intellectually lazy. These 'Romantics', as they were called, wanted a revolution in ideas and in all the arts. Some wanted political revolution, too. They looked for inspiration in wild, remote places, raging winds and waves, in dreams, nightmares, drugs and madness, in glowing sunsets and eerie moonlit nights; and in tales of mystery, magic, love – and horror – collected from faraway lands. Vampires – of course! – became a favourite topic for their works. There were Romantic vampire books, poems, plays, paintings – and even a vampire opera.

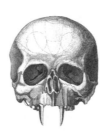

1748

Translated from the German, this is an extract from the first European poem to describe a vampire:

. . . And while you are softly sleeping
I shall creep up to you
And drain your life's blood away.
Ahh! How you will be shivering
Because I will be kissing you
And carrying you through the gates of death,
Horror-struck, in my chilly arms . . .

from 'The Vampire'
Heinrich August Ossenfelder (Austria)

1797

From one of Germany's greatest poets:

These verses tell of a young girl who lived long ago, in Greece. Born into a pagan family, she is promised as a bride to a young man. While she grows up, her family become Christians and cancel the marriage. Soon, she dies. Years later, her promised bridegroom arrives, and is welcomed by her parents. They suggest that he marries her sister, instead. He goes to bed – and is visited by the dead young girl, the Bride of Corinth. He begs her to become his wife, but she refuses. At last she agrees, but there is a terrible price to pay:

I am forced to wander from my grave
To fulfil our broken vow to the Old Gods
To go on loving my lost bridegroom
And to drink his life-blood.
When his life has ended
I must hurry onwards
And seek vengeance by killing other young lovers.
   (To the young man)
'Handsome youngster! You must die!'

from 'The Bride of Corinth'
Johann Wolfgang von Goethe

1813

The most famous Romantic poet in the world – Lord Byron – not only wrote about vampires, but was suspected of being one, as well! Here is just a taste (ha!) of his writing:

This poem was set in the Turkish Ottoman Empire. To Byron's readers, Turkey was a fabulous, unknown land, full of delights – and horrors. In Byron's poem, the Giaour (Unbeliever) has killed his rival. He is condemned to rot in hell, but first he must roam the earth as a vampire, doomed to destroy all those he loves.

> ...But first, on earth as Vampire sent,
> Thy corse[1] shall from its tomb be rent:
> Then ghastly haunt thy native place,
> And suck the blood of all thy race;
> There from thy daughter, sister, wife,
> At midnight drain the stream of life;
> Yet loathe the banquet which perforce[2]
> Must feed thy livid living corse...

from 'The Giaour'
George Gordon, Lord Byron (Britain)

1. corse: corpse.
2. perforce: through necessity.

Here is the outline of a story written by Byron's
private doctor, Polidori. He 'borrowed' the idea
from Byron, and based his vampire hero
(or villain?) on him. It's a winning mixture of sex
and celebrity:

A mysterious nobleman with a face 'of deadly
hue' befriends a young man. They go
travelling, but quarrel because the noble
breaks a woman's heart and kills her. In
Greece the young man falls in love with a local
girl, who tells him old legends about vampires.
But the nobleman lures the girl into the woods
at night. The young man goes to find her:

There was no colour upon her cheek, not even upon
her lip; yet there was a stillness about her face that
seemed almost as attaching as the life that once dwelt
there: upon her neck and breast was blood, and upon
her throat were the marks of teeth having opened the
vein: to this the men pointed, crying, simultaneously
struck with horror, 'A Vampyre! a Vampyre!'

Worse is to follow. Not believing the local
superstitions, the young man agrees to rejoin
the mysterious noble on his travels. They are

attacked by bandits, and the nobleman is fatally wounded. Before he dies, he makes the young man swear to keep silent about their adventures for a year and a day. Why the secrecy? At long last, the young man understands: the nobleman brings death to every woman he touches, but he can't stop loving them.

The young man returns to London, and is amazed to meet the nobleman there, looking strong and healthy. Soon the nobleman meets the young man's sister – and she falls in love with him. The young man is frantic with fear, but cannot break his promise of secrecy. The strain of keeping quiet is too great, and he collapses.

It's now a year since the young man gave his promise. Tomorrow his sister will marry the nobleman. The young man still won't speak, but he writes her a warning letter, and then dies, overcome with emotion. Of course, the letter's too late. The unsuspecting sister weds – and the nobleman vampire kills her!

from The Vampyre
John Polidori (England)

Readers, writers...
and libraries

The craze for vampire stories was helped in a rather unlikely way – by polite, quiet, genteel libraries. New 'reading rooms' were set up in cities and towns throughout Europe and North America from around 1700. At first, most readers came from the wealthy middle and upper classes. They paid a subscription (a regular fee); in return they could borrow books, especially novels, which were very popular with women. There were also libraries where working-class men could improve their education by consulting technical books and encyclopaedias; and, by 1900, a great many public libraries set up by governments or wealthy individuals.

Vampire novels and poems borrowed from subscription libraries were often composed by the most respected writers of their day. They had exciting plots, vivid descriptions, and fascinating characters. They told truths about human characters, feelings, hopes and fears. They were classics – unforgettable!

1800

Another outline – of the first Romantic vampire story written in prose:

A young prince marries a beautiful girl, Brunhilda. She is dark-eyed, rosy-cheeked, red-lipped, warm, voluptuous. But she dies. Next, he marries pale, slim, quiet, delicate and refined Swanhilda. She gives him two children, whom he loves, but still he is not happy. He pines for his lovely Brunhilda. So what does he do? Late one night, he goes to the churchyard to meet a very sinister wizard:

The old enchanter sketched a circle around the grave, muttering magic words all the time. Straight away, a howling storm shook the treetops; owls flapped overhead, their shrieks sounded like warnings. The stars hid their gentle light, so that they would not witness the shocking, unholy ritual . . . The tombstone rolled away from the grave . . . the enchanter strewed the gaping hollow with roots and herbs steeped in his most powerful magic. . . .

At last, the coffin is revealed. As the moonlight touches it, the lid bursts open with a mighty shudder. The enchanter pours on blood from a human skull. 'Drink, sleeping one! Drink.'

from Wake not the Dead
Johann Ludwig Tieck (Germany)

What a page-turner! Brunhilda rises from the dead. And yes, she's a vampire...

Too late, our hero remembers the proverb:
'Be careful what you wish for – you may get it.'

Fear of Females

Many stories featuring female vampires warn how the love of a beautiful woman leads to the death of an innocent, but infatuated, man. Their writers were clearly inspired by ancient vampire myths and legends – but also, at least sometimes, by traditional male attitudes towards women.

Until the 20th century, women were thought to be less intelligent and less capable than men – and much less able to control their thoughts, feelings and behaviour. Like animals, women were said to be ruled by their instincts. Some of these instincts – especially passionate love – were deeply dangerous. And female beauty, and the feelings it inspired in men, were never, ever, to be trusted.

One of the strangest descriptions of a beautiful woman was written by art critic Walter Pater (1839–1894). Its subject? A famous painting by Italian artist Leonardo da Vinci: his portrait of Mona Lisa. Pater sees – and fears – her as the eternal feminine:

'She is older than the rocks among which she sits; like the vampire, she has been dead many times and learned the secrets of the grave ...'

Girls: makes you feel kinda powerful, eh?

1822

Vampire stories collected from folklore tend to be short, simple and disturbing, like this one:

Before he died, Harppe gave strict instructions to his wife. He must be buried in front of the kitchen door; that way, he could see all that was going on in his household. His widow faithfully obeyed him, but, after Harppe died, he was often seen around the neighbourhood. He killed several farmworkers, and molested the neighbours so often that no-one dared live in the houses on either side of his.

Only one man, called Olaus Pa, was brave enough to fight the 'sighting'. He struck it a mighty blow with his spear, leaving the blade firmly lodged in its body. The 'sighting' disappeared, but next day, Pa had Harppe's grave opened. He found his spear-blade there, stuck in the corpse, exactly where the 'sighting' had been wounded.

The corpse had not rotted. So they unwrapped it from its shroud, set it on fire, threw the ashes into the sea — and were never troubled by 'sightings' again!

'Harppe the Vampire', from Infernalia
Charles Nodier (France)

1884

Many vampire stories were inspired by traditional beliefs. This one – translated and summarised – is truly tragic:

A dashing young traveller sets off through the mountains to Moldavia. He meets a village family. Hospitable but anxious, they are waiting for Grandfather to return. He has gone to chase away a bandit. Before he left, he warned them, 'If I am not home within ten days, forget that I'm part of your family. Kill me and drive a stake through my heart, because I will have become a *vourdalak* (vampire)'.

Time passes, and it's ten days by the church clock since the old man went away. It's striking now: one, two, three… But who's that over there? Thank God! It's Grandfather. The clock falls silent. 'Has he got home on time?' 'We must hope so! But we cannot be certain.'

The old man staggers in. He's badly wounded – and dreadfully changed. His eyes are 'dull, glazed, deep in their sockets'. Even the farm dog snarls at him.

His grandchildren ask if he found the bandit. 'I killed him!' he growls – and produces the bandit's stinking head from his knapsack!

You can imagine what happens next. One by one, family members die as vampire Grandfather bites them. When the traveller returns next year, he finds their farmstead – and village – deserted. As he looks at the lonely houses, he hears the swish of a woman's skirt, close by. It's Sdenka, the beautiful daughter from the farm – thank goodness, she's still living!

The traveller takes her into his arms. But, as he does, the cross he wears around his neck digs into his chest and scratches him:

The stab of pain that I felt affected me like a ray of light passing though my body. Looking up at Sdenka, I saw for the first time that her features, though still beautiful, were those of a corpse.

And, through the windows, he sees the whole family of vampires waiting outside...

from The Curse of the Vourdalak
Alexis Tolstoy (Russia)

1836

Forbidden love – that's the theme of this vampire story. Gautier, the author, trained as an artist but became one of France's most famous writers. His work was admired for the vivid word-pictures he created – strange, thrilling, gorgeous...

A young priest is tempted by Clarimonde, a beautiful, wicked woman. At first he ignores her. But then he is called to her deathbed, where he gently kisses her body. Astonishingly, his touch brings her back to life, and they run away together. By day, the young man remains a priest, but at night he shares her sinful life of love and luxury. Before long, the young priest grows weak. Yes, she's been drinking his blood! Even so, he vows he'd willingly die for her.

Just in time, he's saved by an old holy man, who drags him away to a churchyard. In an ancient tomb, they find Clarimonde's body. She's been dead for centuries – and now her bones crumble to dust. 'Let my sins be a lesson to all young men!' says the priest, at the end of the story. But that's not why it was so popular...

One morning . . . I cut myself by accident and made quite a deep wound in my finger. It gushed with blood, and a few purple splashes reached Clarimonde [who was in bed, tired and pale]. Her eyes sparkled, and her face glowed with a fierce, savage delight that I had never seen before. . . .

Swift as a cat, agile as a monkey, she leaped out of bed and pounced on my injured hand. In ecstasy, she began to suck the wound, taking her time, savouring every drop. . . . Her green eyes were half-closed, but I could see the narrow slits of their pupils. From time to time, she paused to kiss my hand – then stooped to kiss the wound again, and drink the last few drops of crimson. . . .

Once the bleeding ceased, she stood up. Her eyes shone, her face glowed with rosy health, her hands felt soft and warm. . . . She was more beautiful than ever! . . . 'I'm not going to die!' she cried, wild with joy, and flung her arms around me. 'Now I can love you for a long, long time.'

from La Morte amoureuse *(The Dead Lover)*
Théophile Gautier (France)

Down to earth

However, these elegant horror stories were sometimes too literary and high-flown for straightforward everyday enjoyment. They did not appeal to busy working men – or women – who had not received a literary education, and had no time for the latest intellectual fads and fashions. They wanted good stories – about vampires and anything else scary, scandalous or sentimental. And they got them, from magazines full of short stories, or in weekly and monthly instalments from cheap papers nicknamed 'penny dreadfuls'.

1845–1847

The most famous vampire 'penny dreadful' ran for over two years. A new episode appeared every week. When printed and bound together, they totalled almost 900 pages. How could anyone write so much, so quickly? Some people said the author must be a secret team of writers, working together. But probably not: it is likely that *Varney the Vampire* was created by just one man, James Malcolm Rymer – and that he was also working on nine other stories at the same time!

Trashy yet tragic – and full of confusing contradictions – *Varney* tells the story of a very reluctant vampire:

. . . he would gladly have been more human and lived and died as those lived and died whom he saw around him.

Varney is attacked and left for dead several times. But always, moonlight revives him and he returns to his vampire habits. At last he ends his miserable existence by jumping into a volcano.

You don't look very reluctant to me.

Varney the reluctant vampire

1872

You should know that I, the beautiful, deadly, female vampire Carmilla, also known as Mircalla or Millarca (work it out), shocked readers 25 years before Dracula was ever dreamed of! You haven't heard of the short story in which I'm the star? Well, it's called after me (hooray!), and was created by Joseph Sheridan Le Fanu, an Irish writer who lived from 1814 to 1873 and specialised in horror.

Le Fanu published my book in 1872. In it, he tells how I haunted castles in Austria, befriending innocent young girls, making them fall in love with me – then sucking their blood. They died, of course. Others were disgusted, but I make no apology. The girls were lonely and I was a good friend to them; in return, I needed their blood to survive.

According to Le Fanu, I began life as a great noble lady hundreds of years ago, at a time when my homeland was positively groaning with vampires. I fell in love with a handsome nobleman, but, in spite of this, it was my destiny to turn into one of the living dead after I passed away from everyday human life. For centuries, I escaped detection – I could walk through walls and doors, and transform myself into a swift, sleek, slinky, silent cat – but at long last, I met my doom. One of my young girl victims was saved by a brave hero vampire-hunter. He arranged for my tomb to be opened and my body destroyed. So that was the end of me – or was it?

from Carmilla
Joseph Sheridan Le Fanu (Ireland)

Choose your vampire!

Throughout the 1800s, a growing number of people in Europe and North America learned how to read and write. As their numbers increased, so did the output of vampire stories. Each new writer presented 'their' vampire in a different way, to fit in with their own beliefs, tastes and theories – and to please their readers. Writing about vampires might be literary, philosophical, artistic or simply for entertainment.

1894

A few vampire stories even tried to blend science with the supernatural. This one's weird!

The villain of *The Parasite* by Sir Arthur Conan Doyle (Britain) is a weak, pathetic, ugly, middle-aged, female, psychic vampire. And she's deadly! She does not drink blood, but instead draws the strength from men's minds, to destroy them. Like a parasitic animal or insect (see Chapter 10), she can't live without the energy of others.

Conan Doyle's story was inspired by fashionable late 19th-century spiritualist experiments, when mediums attempted mesmerism (mind-control) or tried to speak with the spirits of dead people. Much later (1924) Doyle also wrote a Sherlock Holmes short story featuring a vampire. In a typical twist, the 'vampire' is shown not to exist. The real villain is an unhappy teenage boy, jealous of his stepmother and her new baby. He attacks the baby with poison darts fired from a blowpipe. The puncture wounds they create look just like vampire bites!

1896

This short story was written just one year before my story was published. And, like mine, it features the new, very risky science of blood transfusion:

Our heroine, a blooming, healthy, lively young girl called Bella, takes a job as paid companion to the immensely aged and wealthy Lady Ducayne. 'I want a strong young woman,' she says. They travel to a grand hotel in Italy, where the old lady spends every winter. Bella's duties are light: just reading and pleasant conversation.

At first, all is delightful. Bella befriends a young English doctor and his sister, but they leave to continue their travels. After they've gone, she begins to feel tired. Perhaps Italy does not suit her? Then, just by chance, she learns that the girls who had her job before her died in the old lady's service!

Soon after, bad dreams begin. Bella's mind reels and shudders. She hears whirring, whirling sounds and strange murmuring voices. Strangely, her arms are covered in little wounds. 'Just mosquito bites!' says the old lady's doctor.

In spring, the young doctor returns and finds Bella thin, pale and exhausted. He's suspicious – and alarmed. He examines her arms – they're not mosquito bites! – and demands to see the old lady. Frail, crooked, just skin and bone, she must be over a hundred. Her sinister doctor sits close by, watchful and threatening. But the young man is brave, clever – and in love. Boldly, he accuses them.

Lady Ducayne admits it all. Yes, she is kept alive by fresh blood transfusions. Her doctor drugs Bella (the dreams!), draws blood while she sleeps (the 'bites'!), then pumps it into the old lady. Earlier girls have died; soon, it will be Bella's turn to fade away.

How to save Bella? The young doctor knows: blackmail and blood money. The transfusions must stop – or else he'll tell the world! – and Bella must be rewarded. Then, when she's well and strong again, they will go back to England and get married!

from Good Lady Ducayne
Mary E. Braddon (Britain)

Chapter Five

The greatest vampire of all?

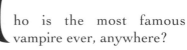

Who is the most famous vampire ever, anywhere?

What a question! Dracula, of course!

89

A great story

Although Dracula was not the first vampire to be described in print, he is by far the best-known. His story combines wild, dramatic locations (Transylvania, now in Romania) with romance and glamour (in the flirtatious shape of pretty Lucy Westenra, his first English victim). It also features a top-rank cast of minor characters: an innocent English traveller; his clever and devoted wife; a young doctor, keen on strange scientific experiments; a dashing English lord; a Continental vampire-hunter; and a brave, loyal American adventurer. There are also three ghastly, ghostly, Brides of Dracula, who hungrily haunt his castle, and a pathetic, raging madman who eats flies and spiders – alive! At the beating, bloody heart of the story stands Count Dracula himself: exotic, hypnotic, proud, noble, charming – and deadly.

Slow starter

Count Dracula was created by Irish theatre manager Bram Stoker (1847–1912), in his fifth book, a horror novel, published in 1897. Stoker's earlier works had not been a great success. But *Dracula*'s racy mix of travel, sex and violence appealed to many readers, and the book won great praise. It did not, however, become a best-seller until after Stoker died. Since then, countless films, books, songs, computer games and websites have been inspired by the Dracula story – and much else besides.

The Land Beyond the Forests

Today, Transylvania is part of the independent nation of Romania. But in the past, it was fought over by empires based in Austria, Hungary and Turkey, as well as being claimed as a homeland by several warring tribes. It is a rugged, very beautiful place in the far east of Europe, surrounded by high mountains. Its name means 'The Land Beyond the Forests' in Latin.

In the late 19th century, when *Dracula* was written, Transylvania was poor and economically undeveloped. It had few cities, roads, railways or modern inventions such as electric light or telephones. Most Transylvanian people lived as shepherds or peasant farmers; many could not read or write. They did not know about the latest scientific discoveries. Some of them probably still believed in magic – and vampires.

Although *Dracula* contains many pages describing Transylvania, Bram Stoker never visited the country. All his information came from books. He mixed fact and fiction to create his own imaginary version of Transylvania: strange, savage and thrillingly dangerous. The magical, primitive, superstitious Transylvania described in *Dracula* never really existed.

Moonlight meeting

In Stoker's book, we first meet Dracula in disguise. He appears as the shadowy coachman who arrives at nightfall to drive an English traveller to a forbidding castle. The Englishman describes the scene:

I could see from the flash of our lamps as the rays fell on them, that the horses were coal-black and splendid animals. They were driven by a tall man, with a long brown beard and a great black hat, which seemed to hide his face from us. I could only see the gleam of a pair of very bright eyes, which seemed red in the lamplight, as he turned to us. . . . the lamplight fell on a hard-looking mouth, with very red lips and sharp-looking teeth, as white as ivory. One of my companions whispered . . . 'Denn die Todten reiten Schnell.'[1]

In spite of his – understandable! – fears, the Englishman agrees to ride in the deadly coach. It is a nightmare journey – wild winds blow, and the coach is attacked by howling, ravenous wolves while, all around, flames

1. *'For the dead travel fast'; from the poem 'Lenore' by Gottfried August Bürger (1747–1794).*

burn with a mysterious blue light on the steep mountainside. The Englishman feels sure that he must die, but at last they reach the castle.

St George's Eve

Before the English traveller sets off for his meeting at the mystery castle, a kindly innkeeper and his wife beg him not to leave them. Fellow travellers say the same. It is St George's Eve – 22 April – and a very dangerous time to stray out of doors. 'Do you know,' they warn, 'that to-night, when the clock strikes midnight, all the evil things in the world will have full sway?'

Traditionally, in Romania, St George's Eve was said to be the time when witches, werewolves and vampires roamed free, and spirits from the world of the dead visited the living. Farmers were especially scared of what these ghosts might do to defenceless farm animals. Often, they spent all night sitting up beside their sheep or cattle.

Dracula's castle

At last, the nightmare drive is over. The traveller has reached Dracula's castle and the ghostly driver helps him climb down – 'His hand . . . seemed like a steel vice that could have crushed mine if he had chosen' – and disappears into the darkness.

Then, after an agonising wait:

There was the sound of rattling chains and the clanking of massive bolts drawn back. A key was turned with the loud grating noise of long disuse, and the great door swung back.

Bran Castle

Although Bram Stoker never visited Transylvania, he was almost certainly thinking of a real castle – Bran Castle – when he described Dracula's residence.

Bran Castle was founded in 1377, and designed as a fortress, with steep, sheer walls rising from rocky cliffs, narrow slits (for firing arrows and guns) instead of windows, and massive gates and drawbridges to keep out invaders. Its purpose was to defend the Transylvanian frontier against attacks from the Ottoman Empire in Turkey, and to protect travellers on an important international trade route leading from eastern Europe towards central Asia.

Bran Castle later became one of the favourite homes of the Romanian royal family. It still exists today, and welcomes tourists.

Dracula's castle
(artist's impression)

As the castle door slowly opens, the English traveller stands trembling. Who – or what – will he meet there? And why were the innkeepers and the other travellers so scared of *it* – or *him*?

Within stood a tall old man, clean-shaven save for a long white moustache, and clad in black from head to foot, without a single speck of colour about him anywhere. . . . He moved impulsively forward, and, holding out his hand, grasped mine with a strength which made me wince . . . it seemed cold as ice, more like the hand of a dead than a living man . . .

Later, the Englishman has the chance to observe Count Dracula more closely:

His face was a strong, a very strong, aquiline, with high bridge of the thin nose and peculiarly arched nostrils, with lofty domed forehead, and hair growing scantily round the temples but profusely elsewhere. His eyebrows were very massive, almost meeting over the nose, and with bushy hair that seemed to curl in its own profusion. The mouth, so far as I could see it under the heavy moustache, was fixed and rather cruel-looking, with peculiarly sharp white teeth. These protruded over the lips, whose remarkable ruddiness showed astonishing vitality in a man of his years. For the rest, his ears were pale, and at the tops extremely pointed. The chin was broad and strong, and the cheeks firm though thin. The general effect was one of extraordinary pallor.

Hitherto I had noticed the backs of his hands as they lay on his knees in the firelight, and they had seemed rather white and fine. But seeing them now close to me, I could not but notice that they were rather coarse, broad, with squat fingers. Strange to say, there were hairs in the centre of the palm. The nails were long and fine, and cut to a sharp point. As the Count leaned over me and his hands touched me, I could not repress a shudder. It may have been that his breath was rank, but a horrible feeling of nausea came over me, which, do what I would, I could not conceal.

In those two paragraphs, Stoker creates the classic image of a vampire, which has lasted for over 100 years.

Later in the book, Stoker gives us a different, but equally threatening, pen-portrait of Dracula. This time, Dracula is in London. He has recently feasted his fill on fresh blood:

. . . a tall, thin man, with a beaky nose and black moustache and pointed beard . . . not a good face. It was hard, and cruel, and sensual, and big white teeth, that looked all the whiter because his lips were so red, were pointed like an animal's . . .

The English traveller (now returned home) sees Dracula, and collapses in terror: 'It is the Count, but he has grown young. My God, if this be so! Oh, my God! My God!'

The man who dreamed up Dracula

Bram (Abraham) Stoker (1847–1912) was born in Dublin, Ireland. His family were prosperous, and he enjoyed a privileged education, first at school, then at Dublin University. As a young child, he was often ill, and spent months in bed. Later, he said that this gave him the chance to develop his imagination.

At university, Stoker studied mathematics, although his real interests were in history, myths, legends and Romantic poetry. After leaving university, Stoker followed his father into a respectable Civil Service career. But he felt restless, and escaped from the dull routine of his work by spending evenings in the theatre. There, he made friends with leading Irish authors, including the master of 19th-century horror-fiction, Sheridan Le Fanu (see page 83), and the artistic, cultured mother of the dramatist Oscar Wilde. She was an expert in Irish folklore. Soon, Stoker began to write his own sinister, supernatural stories.

In 1878, Stoker married Florence Balcombe, an attractive Irish woman with progressive ideas, and moved to London to work as manager of the famous Lyceum Theatre and as personal secretary to superstar actor Henry Irving. These were busy, exciting and exhausting years, but somehow Stoker found time to go on writing. As well as *Dracula*, he published 12 full-length novels and a great many short stories and newspaper articles.

The Lyceum Theatre closed in 1902 and Henry Irving died in 1905. After this, Stoker became a full-time author, writing non-fiction (*Pesonal Reminiscences of Henry Irving* and

Famous Impostors) as well as novels. But none of his later works achieved the fame – or sales – of *Dracula*. Tired and ill, Bram Stoker died in 1912. He was 64.

Dracula checklist

This is the genuine DRACULA! Don't be deceived by imitations!

- Male, tall, elegant, good manners
- Noble ancestors – kings and warriors
- White hair *and* dark hair
- Sharp teeth and fingernails
- Hairy palms
- Bad breath
- Crawls down walls like a lizard
- Rich, ruthless, commanding
- Well-educated; speaks many languages
- Hundreds of years old
- Grows younger after feasts of blood
- Superhuman strength
- Shape-shifts into wolf, monster dog, or bat
- Creeps through narrow openings as mist or magic dust
- No shadow
- No reflection
- Hypnotises his victims
- Controls wild animals
- Bite turns humans into vampires

Not bad, eh?

> But even so, I have my limitations:

- I can't cross running water.
- I must sleep in a box of earth from my native land.
- I prefer to prowl around after dark.
- I'm not very fond of daylight.
- I can't enter a house without being invited – though once in, I'm there for ever!

A real-life vampire?

Before writing *Dracula*, Bram Stoker spent almost seven years researching. He consulted travel guides, geography books, shipping lists and railway timetables, although he never left England. He read folktales, myths, legends, and a great many horror stories, including earlier books about vampires (see chapter 4). He met a famous east European scholar, and studied the history of Transylvania, taking the name of his villain Dracula from a famous Romanian warrior, Prince Vlad III Ţepeş, who lived nearly 600 years ago.

Vlad's family, like Count Dracula's ancestors in Stoker's book, fought to defend Romania against invaders from Hungary and the Turkish Ottoman Empire. Vlad's father, Vlad II, belonged to a secret brotherhood of warrior knights called the Order of the Dragon. Because of this, Vlad III became known as Vlad Dracula (Vlad, son of the Dragon). But, as Bram Stoker discovered, the Romanian word *dracul* can also mean 'the devil', and 'devil' was sometimes used as a name for vampires.

No-one knows how much Bram Stoker really understood about the historical Vlad III Dracula, who lived from 1431 to 1476. (For example, he sited Vlad/Dracula's homeland and castle in the wrong region of Romania.) In real life, Vlad Dracula, nicknamed Țepeș – 'the Impaler' – is said to have been a cruel psychopath, torturing and killing many thousands of his own people, as well as countless foreign enemies. But this mass slaughter may have been exaggerated, since almost all the descriptions of Vlad's killings were written by hostile observers. Probably, Vlad's aim was to 'purify' his country by

You don't have to believe everything they say about me.

Vlad III Dracula

ridding it of criminals and (regrettably) of foreigners. He also fought fiercely to defend its borders from attack – and to destroy all his royal rivals.

Vlad's own life ended violently. He was turned off the throne and imprisoned for years by his own brother. He escaped, but soon after was assassinated. His grave has never been found. For centuries, he has been honoured as a national hero in Romania – and was never, before Stoker's book, accused of being a vampire.

Tales for the times

Bram Stoker lived at a time (the late 19th century) when Britain was very rich, very powerful, but also very anxious. The British empire covered one quarter of the Earth, but defending its borders was a constant strain – and also very costly. British industries were the envy of the world, but life in British cities was grim, and British workers were demanding higher pay, better working conditions, and political rights. Old, noble families – and the royal family, as well – were criticised for their extravagance and outdated ways of living. Some politicians feared that there might be a revolution!

Horror stories and vampire tales reflected these anxieties, through safe, harmless entertainment. Dracula himself belonged to the old nobility; some people have seen him as a symbol of the rich feeding on the life-blood of the hard-working poor.

Life in industrial cities was often very violent, as well as dirty, smelly, poor and mean. Muggers, robbers and pickpockets lurked in dark alleyways; homeless people, child beggars and prostitutes lingered in slum streets. In 1888, all London was scandalised by a series of brutal, bloody murders. The villain, nicknamed 'Jack the Ripper' (he was never traced), killed his victims – all poor, defenceless young women – in a particularly cruel and bloody way. New cheap newspapers – the latest media craze at that time – delighted in describing the sadistic attacks. It has been suggested that Bram Stoker borrowed some details from the Jack the Ripper story for *Dracula*.

Haunted holidays

Some of the most dramatic episodes in Bram Stoker's *Dracula* are set in the seaside town of Whitby, in north-east England. Stoker spent several holidays there, staying at the old Royal Hotel, and reading books about vampires and Transylvania. He also talked to Whitby sailors about past events in the town. One of the most exciting was a wreck, when a large Russian cargo ship had run aground.

Stoker's heroine, the clever, dependable Mina, and her pretty, flighty friend Lucy, go to Whitby on holiday. They enjoy walking though the historic streets, along the scenic cliffs and beside the busy harbour. They stroll past the ancient, ruined Abbey and through the tranquil, but spooky, graveyard. An old man entertains them with stories, and predicts that he will soon be buried there.

All goes well until, one night, there is a terrible storm. A Russian ship is washed ashore in the harbour. The only man on board is the captain; he has lashed himself to the wheel, is clutching a crucifix, and seems to have died from fear. There is nothing else on the ship except for a huge black dog that leaps ashore and runs away – and a great many boxes full of earth. Soon after, the old man is found dead with a look of terror on his face, and various dogs in Whitby are savagely killed at night.

Lucy begins to sleepwalk. Mina is worried and follows her wanderings. She finds Lucy stretched over a tomb in the graveyard. A strange dark shape is bending over her, with eyes glowing blood-red…

Whitby and the Goth scene

You must read Bram Stoker's book[1] to find out what happens to Lucy and her loyal friend Mina. But it's no secret that Bram Stoker's *Dracula* has turned Whitby into a major tourist destination. *Dracula* fans flock there, together with thousands of Goths. They take guided tours to places mentioned in Bram Stoker's story. They walk to the spot where Stoker gazed out over the sea to imagine the wreck of the haunted ship *Demeter*. (The site is now marked by a memorial seat, erected by the Town Council!)

Today, Whitby has Goth shops, Goth cafés and a Goth hotel. Twice a year, in April and October (near Halloween, of course!), it hosts international Goth festivals, with concerts, street markets, charity Goth football, prizes for Goth costumes, and various Dracula-inspired happenings all around the town.

Stamp of approval

In 2008, the UK Post Office paid an unexpected tribute to Dracula – and to Whitby – by issuing a special postage stamp in honour of the town's most famous vampire. Priced at 48p, then the standard rate for international letters, it portrayed actor Christopher Lee as a charming, sinister Dracula.

1. Or read the graphic version of it in Book House's Graffex series.

Just a bite?
Dinner with Dracula

Yes, vampires feast on fresh blood. But if you were invited to dinner with a vampire, what else might you expect to find on your plate and in your glass?

Some of my favourites!

Starters

Let me recommend:

• **Blood sausage** The deepest, darkest, direst red, this special sausage is made with fresh blood thickened with breadcrumbs, oatmeal, barley or rice. Then it's blended with chopped fat, and flavoured with onions, herbs and spices – or even (in South America) chocolate and dried fruit. Finally, it's stuffed into animal intestines, ready for cooking.

My castle chef can serve it just how you like it:

• Irish and Scottish-style, *black pudding*: sliced and fried, with bacon and egg. Or dipped in batter then deep-fried, with chips.

• French-style, *boudin noir*: boiled, with stewed apples and mashed potatoes.

• German-style, *Blutwurst*: hot-smoked and dried, then thinly sliced, with pickles.

• Spanish-style, *morcilla*: grilled or barbecued. (Warning: may contain nuts! Almonds and pine-nuts are Spanish favourites.)

• Caribbean-style, *bloedworst* or *black pudding*: boiled, with hot chilli sauce.

Don't fancy sausages? Then try:

• **Svartsoppa** (black soup, from Sweden): Made with blood, vinegar, meat stock and, sometimes, sliced apples or pears.

• **Veriohukainen** (blood pancakes, from Finland): Wafer-thin pancakes made with pig's blood, beer, eggs, rye flour, onion, molasses (raw sugar syrup) and spices.

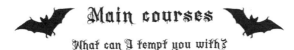

Main courses

What can I tempt you with?

• **Coq au vin** The name of this classic French dish means 'rooster in wine'. It is made by gently stewing an old, tough chicken in rich red wine, together with onions and mushrooms. The chicken's blood is added just before serving to thicken the gravy.

• **Xie doufou** From China, this 'blood tofu' is fresh pig or duck blood left to congeal (thicken) naturally, then cut into neat cubes or slices. It is simmered in a spicy soup or stir-fried with vegetables.

• **Steak au bleu** Popular in the USA and Europe, steak *au bleu* (very rare or 'blue' steak) is a big, juicy beefsteak, lightly browned on the outside but raw, bluish-purple and dripping with blood-coloured juices in the centre.

• **Laab** This refreshing salad originates from Laos, in east Asia. It contains minced meat, raw or cooked, mixed with toasted rice and vegetables. Fresh blood is poured on top.

 ## Desserts

To finish your meal, what about a lovely, luscious dessert?

• **Red velvet cake** Very rich, extremely chocolatey, sinfully sweet, dark brownish-red (like stale blood!) and light as a feather, this cake is also known as 'devil's food'. (And what does that tell us?!) It's made from eggs, butter, sugar, flour, milk and pure cocoa powder. Its airy texture comes from extra baking soda (sodium bicarbonate) in the recipe; this also turns the cocoa an appetising blood-red.

Once baked, the cake is usually decorated with sugary-white frosting that makes each slice look like a freshly cut slab of quivering flesh and blood. It is best served in small portions, with tea or strong coffee.

Watching your weight? Don't have a sweet tooth? Then try this blood-red fresh fruit dessert. It's disgustingly healthy!

• **Blood-orange salad** We choose selected blood oranges to delight you. These are rare, beautiful oranges from southern Italy, California and Spain. Full of taste – and goodness – their juice looks like freshly flowing blood.

Blood oranges have an orange skin tinged with speckles of fiery blood-red, deep purple flesh, and a fabulous flavour – like raspberries!

You can even make this simple treat yourself, by just slicing the oranges and sprinkling with icing sugar (if liked) and mint leaves. Best served thrillingly, chillingly ice-cold.

113

Beverages

I only drink blood, of course, but what do you fancy?

My most decadent guests like to sip a 'Bloody Mary' cocktail before their meal. Made with tomato juice, vodka and ice, it tastes terrifying – and looks, well, bloody. But for most diners, a less extreme choice is the historic, deep-red wine known as 'Bull's Blood'.

Bull's Blood is made from grapes grown in Hungary, close to my homeland, Transylvania.

Too strong for your taste? There are plenty more blood-red drinks to choose from...

• **Sangria** If you're over 18 and in party mood, try this light, summery drink from Spain. Made from red wine and oranges (blood oranges are best, naturally!), it takes its name from *sangre*, the Spanish word for 'blood'.

Under 18? Then try the alcohol-free but blood-red mixtures on pages 116 and 117!

The legend of Bull's Blood

In 1552, invading armies from Turkey attacked a Hungarian fortress town called Eger. This town was in the middle of a famous vine-growing district, where a strong red wine was made from deep purple grapes. As the Turks surrounded their city, the men of Eger drank this wine to make themselves feel brave before fighting.

The grape-skins in the wine stained their beards a deep blood-red, and so a wild rumour spread throughout the country. People said that the men of Eger were killing mighty bulls and drinking their blood, to get superhuman strength in battle. (They also said – quite wrongly – that 'Bull's Blood' helped to cure stomach diseases.) The Turkish armies were so frightened by this news that they retreated. Eger was saved!

Today, dark red wine from Eger in Hungary is still called *Bikaver* ('Bull's Blood'). But no-one claims that it has special strengthening powers!

Vampire smoothie

To share with a thirsty friend, you'll need:

- 1 banana
- 1 ripe peach
- 1 mugful of any fresh, ripe, red or purple fruits or berries: e.g. raspberries, strawberries, blackberries, blackcurrants or blueberries
- 2 scoops ice cream (raspberry ripple looks like flesh and blood!)
- Fresh orange juice

1. Peel the banana and chop it into chunks.

2. Peel the peach and remove the stone – see how bloody the flesh looks around it! Cut peach flesh into chunks.

3. Rinse the berries in water and remove any stalks.

4. Whizz banana, peach and berries in a blender or food processor (under adult supervision). Add a little orange juice if the mixture gets too thick.

5. Pour into glasses. Add ice cubes if liked, and top with ice cream.

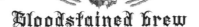

Bloodstained brew

For each person, you will need:

- 1 tablespoon undiluted blackcurrant squash or syrup
- Fresh orange juice
- Ice cubes
- Sparkling water

1. Pour blackcurrant syrup into the bottom of a glass.

2. Add 2 or 3 ice cubes.

3. **Slowly and very carefully,** pour orange juice on top of the ice, so that the purple blackcurrant streaks rise up and mix with it, like blood.

4. If the mixture tastes too strong, add some sparkling water.

Save some for me!

Other ways of eating blood

Far away from Dracula's castle, people in many different parts of the world have also traditionally eaten fresh blood. They have done this *not* because they are vampires, but as a way of getting essential nourishment in very harsh environments.

Too poor to buy meat to eat, herdsmen and their families in East Africa, Scotland, Tibet, Finland and many other places have all taken small amounts of blood from their living animals[1] to drink raw or mix with grains and cook, like porridge.

So as not to harm their animals – their main source of wealth – herdsmen take blood only from low-pressure veins, and try to make sure that the wounds heal cleanly. The blood provides vital protein, vitamins and minerals to supplement their near-starvation diet. And, if the animals are well fed, their bones soon produce fresh blood to make up the loss.

1. Cattle in Africa and Scotland, yaks in Tibet, reindeer in Finland.

Chapter Seven

"We are many..."
Could you spot a vampire?

Most of us like to think that we know what a vampire looks like – deathly-pale skin, deep red lips, fangs dripping with blood – but this image only dates from the 1890s, when Bram Stoker wrote his famous novel, *Dracula*. Earlier descriptions of vampires report many different appearances.

> They seek me here, they seek me there...

WANTED

DEAD OR UNDEAD
COUNT DRACULA

Late of Transylvania, Now ROAMING THE WORLD!!

Distinguishing features:

- Aristocratic appearance · Haunted, burning eyes ·
- Pale skin · Fangs · Red, sensuous lips ·
- Sharp claw-like fingernails ·
- May be trace of blood at corner of mouth ·
- Wears black a lot ·

WARNING: Do not approach this man.
He is dangerous.

So, could you always be sure to spot a vampire? Try this quiz! How many of the following features have been said to belong to vampires **before** I was written about?

- Plump and well fed
- Swollen, bloated body
- Red or purple in the face
- Bleeding from nose, ears, mouth or any other body opening
- Body not decayed
- Dressed in a shroud (burial sheet)
- Unusually hairy
- Left eye cannot be closed after death
- Old skin flaking away in tomb; new skin growing underneath
- Twisted feet
- Flesh-eating, not blood-sucking
- Throws things and makes mysterious noises like a poltergeist
- Plays malicious tricks
- Attacks family members, not strangers
- Makes love to victims instead of killing them
- Lives for ever

ANSWER:
All of them!

Blood-sucking monsters feature in traditional myths and legends from all round the world. Surprisingly, most are women. Of course, they lack my deadly masculine charm, but they have their own ways of finding blood...

Femmes Fatales

In Bram Stoker's novel *Dracula* (see Chapter 5), Jonathan Harker, an innocent traveller, goes exploring in Dracula's castle. He falls asleep, and wakes to find a beautiful young woman (one of Dracula's vampire brides) very, very close beside him:

I was afraid to raise my eyelids, but looked out and saw perfectly under the lashes. The girl went on her knees, and bent over me, simply gloating. There was a deliberate voluptuousness which was both thrilling and repulsive, and as she arched her neck, she actually licked her lips like an animal . . .

Lower and lower went her head as the lips went below the range of my mouth and chin and seemed about to fasten on my throat ... I closed my eyes in a languorous ecstasy and waited — waited with beating heart. I could feel the soft, shivering touch of the lips on the supersensitive skin of my throat, and the hard dents of two sharp teeth, just touching and pausing there.

That's quite enough of that!

Phew! Let's see what some other female — and male — vampires get up to. A word of warning: these are just some of them — and they don't all look like me!

An A-Z of vampires worldwide

Asanbosam (West Africa) With hooks for feet and iron teeth and claws, this vampire hangs from rainforest trees, ready to pounce.

Bhuta (India) This name, which means 'ghost' or 'spirit', sometimes refers to a misty, murderous vampire-ghost that casts no shadow as it floats through the dark night-time air. But don't be deceived by its lack of substance – it is a hungry hunter which loves to devour humans. Reborn from the corpse of a man who led a wicked life, or who died young and horribly, it cannot rest on earth until it finds another body to enter. Then, from the inside, it takes control and consumes it – alive!

Blutsauger (south Germany) Cold, clammy, deathly pale and locked in a zombie-like trance, it prowls through the night, seeking its fill of warm blood to bring it back to life.

Cihuateteo (Mexico) The ancient Aztecs believed that these skull-faced spirits of women who died in childbirth haunted lonely crossroads at night, preying on travellers.

Empusa (ancient Greece) Demon daughter of Hecate, goddess of the Underworld. She drank blood from young men as they slept.

Jiangshi (China) Spirits of people who have suffered a violent death, they search for fresh corpses to live in. They attack their victims by ripping off their heads or tearing them limb from limb. They are covered in green furry mould and hop on one leg. A few are extra-dangerous: they can fly.

Kallikantzaros (Greece) According to traditional beliefs, Greek children born between Christmas Day and Epiphany (6 January in the modern Western calendar) are destined to become vampires. Each birthday, they go in search of victims and rip them to shreds with long, cruel, talon-like fingernails.

Lamia (ancient Greece) Lamia was queen of Libya in North Africa. She fell in love with Zeus, king of the Greek gods, and had his child, but the baby was taken away by Zeus's jealous wife, Hera. For ever after, Lamia could not bear the sight of happy parents and children. She – and many women friends – became horrible monsters, half-woman, half-snake.

Lamia

The poem 'Lamia' by English poet John Keats (1795–1821) tells the story of a young man who falls in love with a beautiful, blood-sucking monster. She speaks very sweetly, as if 'through bubbling honey', to entice her prey. To win the young man's heart, Lamia disguises herself as a woman, but he dies of terror at their wedding when she turns back into a snake:

She was a gordian[1] shape of dazzling hue,[2]
Vermilion-spotted, golden, green, and blue;
Striped like a zebra, freckled like a pard,[3]
Eyed like a peacock, and all crimson barr'd;[4]
And full of silver moons, that, as she breathed,
Dissolv'd, or brighter shone, or interwreathed
Their lustres[5] with the gloomier tapestries[6] –
So rainbow-sided, touch'd with miseries,
She seem'd, at once, some penanced[7] lady elf,
Some demon's mistress, or the demon's self.
Upon her crest[8] she wore a wannish[9] fire
Sprinkled with stars, like Ariadne's[10] tiar:[11]
Her head was serpent, but ah, bitter-sweet!
She had a woman's mouth with all its pearls[12]
   complete:
And for her eyes: what could such eyes do there
But weep, and weep, that they were born so fair?

1. gordian: knotted, twining.   2. hue: colour.   3. pard: leopard.
4. barr'd: striped.   5. lustres: shining.
6. tapestries: patterns on her skin.   7. penanced: sinful.
8. crest: forehead.   9. wannish: pale, ghostly.
10. Ariadne: an ancient Greek heroine.   11. tiar: tiara or crown
12. pearls: teeth.

Langsuir (Malaysia) The bitter, tragic, vengeful, still-living spirit of a woman who has died giving birth to a child. Her lovely long black hair hides a horrible mouth at the back of her head, which she uses to suck blood from sleeping babies.

Lilith or **Lilitu** (Middle East) A beautiful, deadly, bird-footed female monster, who lives in the desert and rides on storm-clouds. Some say she is the wife of the devil. She preys on babies, especially girls, and drinks their blood.

Loogaroo (Caribbean) This Voodoo vampire woman has a terrible duty – to supply the devil with fresh warm blood every night. If she cannot steal blood from another living creature, the devil will drain her own blood from her. Her name comes from the French for 'werewolf': *loup-garou*.

Manananggaal (Philippines) A beautiful older woman who can split herself in half and sprout wings from her upper body. She flies at night to suck the hearts and blood from pregnant women and their unborn babies.

Mullo (eastern Europe) In the past, the Roma people of eastern Europe believed

127

that dead ancestors would return to drink the blood of living family members who had harmed them, or not showed proper respect at their funerals.

Nachtzehrer (north Germany) Famously greedy, these Night Destroyers don't just drink blood, but rise up from their tombs to eat the flesh of their victims as well. If they can't find anyone living to devour, they chew off their own hands and feet and munch their own burial clothes.

Ramanga (Madagascar) A vampire outlaw who drinks the blood of noblemen – and eats their nail-clippings!

Strix (plural **striges**; ancient Rome) Blood-sucking, flesh-eating monsters that fly at night. They bring bad luck to all who see them. Legends tell how they are descended from a woman who married a bear and was turned into an owl as a punishment for cannibalism.

Ustrel (Bulgaria) These are the spirits of children who are born on Saturdays and die before they can be baptised into the Christian faith. Ancient legends tell how, nine days after burial, they rise from the grave to feast on the blood of sheep or cows.

Vetala (India) Grim spirits that haunt the shadowy world between the living and the dead. They lurk in graveyards, seeking dead bodies to inhabit for a while. Like bats, they hang upside-down from trees. They can see everything: past, present and future. It is said that an ancient Indian king tried to capture them, to use as slaves.

Yara-ma-yha-who (Australia) A small man-like creature with a huge mouth and blood-sucking tips to its fingers. It lurked in fig trees, ready to jump down and drain the blood from unwary travellers.

Here's another talent of mine that you may not have been aware of. Who needs stairs?

Want to try living death as a vampire? Let a
vampire bite you. That's the simplest way!

Sir Philip Burne-Jones painted
The Vampire in 1897 – the very same
year as Bram Stoker's *Dracula*.

Chapter Eight

A fate worse than death

Becoming a vampire

Traditionally, the quickest way to become a vampire was to be bitten by one. But it's a good job that vampires don't bite that many people, otherwise the world would soon be completely full of them! A mathematician has calculated that if the first vampire had started his career in 1600 and bitten just one person each month, it would have taken only two and a half years for the entire human population to be turned into vampires.[1] Then who would they have fed on?

1. http://blogs.techrepublic.com.com/geekend/?p=377

But biting is not the only way. Here are some other methods...

1. Find an unburied corpse to inhabit

The idea that humans are made of two parts, a body and a soul, is common to many cultures. Traditionally, the body is the 'bad' or 'weak' part. Formed from flesh and blood, it belongs to the natural world, and, like all other living things, from the tallest trees to the tiniest insects, it has a limited lifespan. Sooner or later, it is doomed to wither, rot and decay. In contrast, the soul, or spirit, is the better part of each person. It guides or controls the body, and, according to many traditional beliefs, desires only to seek peace, or good, or God.

Many traditions teach that the spirit leaves a dead body and lives on. It may rest quietly, go to heaven or hell, be reborn in a new living creature, or watch over living family members. But not all spirits are able to pass away in peace. If they have lived wickedly, died violently, or been cursed, enchanted or murdered, their souls will wander restlessly on earth. The same fate will befall them if funeral ceremonies have not been performed properly.

These homeless, restless spirits have been feared all round the world. They may be angry, vengeful, jealous, wistful – or simply desperate to go on living in any way they can. They may haunt lonely places as ghosts, or disturb happy houses as poltergeists. If they find an unguarded corpse, they may take possession of it, and turn it into a zombie (a mindless walking monster) – or a vampire, hungry for life-giving blood.

Feet First

Simply passing from one state of being (alive) to another (dead) was said to give people dangerous powers. In many parts of England, a corpse was always carried feet-first out of the building in which it had died – otherwise its spirit would return to haunt the place.

Bloodshed at funerals

In some remote parts of the Highlands of Scotland, until around 1800, it was the custom for two male friends of the dead person to fight at the funeral until one of them began to bleed. This was a way of offering blood to the spirit of the dead person, to give it strength for the Afterlife.

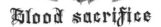

Blood sacrifice

The ancient Greeks and Romans believed that the spirits of the dead lived on in a cold, dark, gloomy Underworld. These gibbering ghosts had life and strength for as long as living people remembered them – or fed them, best of all with blood.

The ancient Greek poet Homer described how the brave hero Odysseus dared to go down into the Underworld to ask advice from the spirits of the dead. To summon them, Odysseus killed a fine black ram – and the pale, greedy ghosts flocked to drink its blood:

'I promised the sacrifice, then slashed the lamb and its mother, letting their black blood spurt into the pit I had dug. Then the dead souls streamed out of Hell. They surged from all around, eager to find the pit, shrieking and crying. I felt sick with fear. I crouched with my sword in my hand, trying to keep the ghostly crowd away.

from The Odyssey
Homer

2. Be accused of witchcraft or black magic

Before modern science, most people believed in magic. They had no other way to explain the puzzling and frightening world around them. They also believed in shamans, holy healers, witches and wizards: people who could contact unseen magic forces, and use them to help – or to harm.

All these people with supernatural skills were admired, but also feared. Where did their powers come from? Were they perhaps in league with the devil? And who knew when they might turn their magic against people who had offended them? Often, too, they used forbidden bodily substances, such as blood or urine, in their spells. Like vampires, they meddled with life-giving forces – and, because of this, they might be punished by a very unquiet life after death.

Stemming the Flow

Some Celtic traditional healers were said to have the power to stop any bleeding, however serious. They did this by reciting magic spells over the patient. If that did not work, they made the patient eat their own blood, collected from their bleeding wound, then boiled, dried and powdered.

3. Break holy laws

There was another, deeper reason why spirits might be condemned to an unhappy life as vampires. It was a punishment for breaking religious laws, or spending time with 'unclean' things, such as corpses. Anyone who did this – whatever their faith – ran the risk of being treated as an outcast, or even a vampire.

Why was religious disobedience such a crime? Because it was dangerous! Breaking holy law was a threat to the good order of the whole universe. If you believed – as most people did – that the laws of nature and of human life were made by God or the gods, then breaking them was deeply disrespectful, and threatened the safety of the whole planet.

Unclean!

In eastern England, people believed that if a dead body was carried across a field on its way to burial, crops would not grow in that field for many years.

Bad luck!

In many countries, a corpse on a ship is said to bring bad weather.

4. Die in childbirth

Childbirth is a dangerous time. In the past, it was the chief cause of death among young women. To die while giving birth to a new life was tragic – but also confusing, strange and sinister.

A woman who died this way might naturally expect to be sorrowful at leaving her husband and her newborn baby. But in many countries, she was also seen as jealous, resentful, eager for revenge – and keen to come back to life.

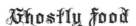

Ghostly Food

In north-western India, a woman who died in childbirth or from abuse by her family was said to turn into a *churel* (angry ghost). She would come back to haunt the family home, and dry up the blood of all male family members. Or she might become a *dakini*, a follower of the bloodthirsty goddess Kali. She would tempt young men away from home at night with ghostly meals. If they ate her food, they returned home the next morning old, grey-haired, wrinkled and exhausted.

White Ladies

In Brazil, many places are said to be haunted by a disturbing *Dama Branca* (White Lady), a pale, bloodless, hungry young woman in a long, flowing white gown. Most White Ladies are ghosts of women who died in childbirth, or who were killed by violent husbands or fathers. But one chilling tale tells how a young wife who fell in love with a slave was murdered by her jealous husband. He killed the slave then locked the lady away, with no food except slices of flesh from the dead slave's corpse. So she starved and died – and returned to prey on her husband.

5. Die from an infectious disease

If people catch the same sickness as you, they will blame you, long after you are dead, and perhaps call you a vampire. For many centuries, victims of dangerous diseases – leprosy, plague, tuberculosis and more recently AIDS – have been treated as outcasts. Sometimes they have also inspired a morbid fascination with sickness and death, and superstitious fears.

My story, as told by Bram Stoker, first became really popular after a pandemic of deadly flu swept round the world in 1918–1920. It killed between 50 and 100 million people; most were young and healthy. Their symptoms included bleeding under the skin and from the ears and nose.

Perhaps readers made a connection between the terrible death-toll all around them, and Bram Stoker's book?

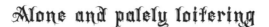

Alone and palely loitering

In 1818, young English poet John Keats realised that he was dying of tuberculosis. The next year, he wrote a poem, 'La Belle Dame Sans Merci' (The Beautiful Lady Without Mercy), telling how a young man met a lovely, wild-eyed lady, who took him to her mysterious cave and kissed him:

> And there she lullèd me asleep,
>   And there I dream'd – Ah! woe betide![1]
> The latest[2] dream I ever dream'd
>   On the cold hill's side.
>
> I saw pale kings and princes too,
>   Pale warriors, death-pale were they all;
> They cried – 'La Belle Dame sans Merci
>   Hath thee in thrall!'[3]
>
> I saw their starved lips in the gloam,[4]
>   With horrid warning gapèd[5] wide,
> And I awoke and found me here,
>   On the cold hill's side.

Was the Beautiful Lady a vampire, or a symbol of Keats's illness? Both, probably.

1. woe betide: dreadful news!
2. latest: last (the young man is dead – but still speaking).
3. Hath thee in thrall: has got you in her clutches.
4. gloam: twilight.
5. gapèd: gaping.

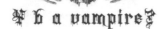

¥ b a vampire?

Would you qualify? Take this quick quiz!

Do you want:

• Forbidden thrills?	YES/NO
• Sense of power?	YES/NO
• Drama and excitement?	YES/NO
• Change of shape?	YES/NO
• Love – or imagined love?	YES/NO
• Hope of everlasting youth?	YES/NO

BUT could you also cope with:

• Losing control of your body, spirit or soul?	YES/NO
• Exchanging normal looks for a ghastly glamour?	YES/NO
• Growing immoral and immodest?	YES/NO
• Preying upon your friends?	YES/NO
• Becoming a parasite?	YES/NO
• Being hated and feared?	YES/NO
• Being undead, for ever?	YES/NO

More 'yes'
than 'no'?
Welcome,
stranger!

More 'no'
than 'yes'?
Stay away!

Back from the brink

How do you stop a corpse becoming a vampire?
These remedies come from many different parts
of the world.

- Bury the body upside down.
- Put a broken egg and an iron nail beneath the coffin.
- Stick hawthorn twigs all around the grave.
* Stop dogs, cats or any other animals jumping over the dead body.
- Wind red woollen thread (looks like blood!) round the burial ground.
- If the body is injured, pour boiling water on its wounds.
- Leave coins or valuable objects (knives, farm tools) with the body. Evil spirits will steal these and leave the body alone.
- Cut the tendons behind the knees; this will stop the dead body standing, walking or running.
- Bury the body with a crucifix.
- Place red flowers on the grave, and four iron nails around it.
- Carry the corpse out of the house by a window or a side door. This will confuse its vampire spirit, which won't be able to find the front door.
- If all else fails, shoot a bullet into the coffin, before the body is buried. After burial might be too late...

So many people claim to have seen vampires that these precautions can't have worked very well!

VAMPIRE-PROOF
YOUR HOME!

Seen bats fluttering?   Heard wolves howling?

• Feeling tired, drained and pale? •

ASK THE EXPERTS!

Van Helsing Pest Control Services can show
you how to keep even the oldest, crumbliest,
spookiest house safely VAMPIRE-FREE!!!

MONEY BACK
if not satisfied★

We use only the finest organic garlic and
☞ genuine boxwood crucifixes. ☜

* Offer applies only if you survive.

** Always read the small print.

10 ways to keep vampires away

1. Wear or hold a crucifix (a little carving of Jesus on the Cross).

2. Carry a bottle of holy water (water blessed by a priest).

3. Seal doors, locks and windows with Communion wafers (holy bread, used in Church services).

Christians believe that their God is greater than all the powers of darkness – including vampires.

4. Hang wreaths of garlic flowers at your windows and doors, drape them around your bed, and, if you're feeling really frightened, wear a necklace of them, too.

Garlic's very pretty – but extremely smelly. Its pungent odour is enough to keep almost anything away! More important, magicians say that garlic interferes with magnetic forces. That would certainly confuse wild birds and animals – they use the earth's magnetic field to navigate. It probably disorientates flying vampires as well.

5. For double-strength protection, eat raw garlic, carry garlic in your pockets, and hang plaits of dried garlic throughout your house, not only in your kitchen.

6. Carry twigs from the graceful rowan tree that grows on mountains throughout Europe. Plant one in your garden too.

Rowan berries are bright red, like blood, and everyone knows that a rowan tree keeps witches – and, with luck, vampires – away from your door.

7. Plant the biggest, prickliest thistles you can find all round your house, together with thorny wild roses.

Well, would you like to fight your way through them? Vampires need blood. We don't want to lose it though cuts and scratches!

8. Sprinkle salt about.

For centuries, it's been used in rituals of cleansing and healing. And, mixed with cold water, it's brilliant at removing bloodstains.

9. Carry cold iron.

Since Roman times, iron knives, and sharp iron objects such as nails, have been used to scare away supernatural creatures. And, traditionally, touching iron brings safety or good luck.

10. Scatter seeds.

We vampires are tidy creatures – and we don't like to waste anything. So, if you scatter seeds in front of us, we just have to stop and pick them all up – and that can take ages!

There's another reason, too. Seeds are full of potential life. If you plant and water them, they will grow. We vampires don't eat plants, but we are always on the look-out for fresh supplies of life and energy.

Chapter Nine

Mad, bad and dangerous to know?

Almost everywhere, in every age, drinking human blood has been shocking, sinful and forbidden. However, in extreme conditions, some real-life people dared to drink blood. What were their reasons? Some hoped to get strength from the dead, or magic powers over the living. Some wanted revenge on their enemies, or longed for a cure for sickness. A few were frantic with grief. Many hoped to contact dead ancestors or meet mighty gods. Others were simply mad or bad – and extremely dangerous. Beware, as you read this chapter: their stories can be very nasty!

Precious blood

An eyewitness report from 19th-century Ireland:

At the execution of a notable traitor in Limerick ... I saw an old woman, which was his foster-mother, take up his head ... and suck up all the blood that ran out, saying that the earth was not worthy to drink it, and therewith she steeped[1] her face and breast and tore her hair, crying out and shrieking most terribly ...

from The Golden Bough
J. G. Frazer

1. steeped: soaked.

Did you know? Until the 1800s, when vampire stories – like mine! – became fashionable, few of these past blood-suckers actually called themselves vampires.

Cruel countess

Who was the most bloodthirsty of all? Probably Countess Erzsébet (Elizabeth) Báthory, from Hungary. Born in 1560 to an ancient noble family, she was immensely grand, extremely rich and very beautiful. She was clever and capable, managing her husband's farms and castles while he was away at war. She was friends with kings and princes; she travelled; she studied science. But, even if only half of what was said about her is true, she was also a mass-murderer. At her trial, she was accused of killing 650 young girls – and enjoying it.

Báthory's victims were female servants, farm workers, and young girls sent to live in her castles to be educated. If they displeased her, she beat them, scratched them with 'claw-like' nails, stuck pins in them – or had them stripped and thrown out of the castle into the snow, where they froze and died. She was also reported to bite them.

In 1610, Báthory was arrested after a young noblewoman died in her castle. Báthory claimed that it was suicide – but she was found guilty of murder and locked away in a prison cell in her own castle, where she died four years later.

Báthory is often called 'a female Dracula'. But was she a vampire? No – although she probably did suck blood from her victims' wounds. The most scandalous story about her, that she bathed in young girls' blood to keep her skin smooth and beautiful, did not appear until 100 years after her death. It may have been invented by her family's many enemies – or it just might be true…

2500–1200 BC

A deal's a deal! Promise loyalty to your brothers, and seal your bargain with human blood! (But don't try this at home.)

Members of prehistoric tribes drank blood to bond with one another or to confirm agreements. Around 2500 BC, Greek travellers watched while Scythians in central Asia made solemn a promise, then stabbed themselves, poured their blood into a bowl, mixed it with wine, and drank it. Later, around AD 1200, Mongol tribes, who ruled a vast empire stretching from China to Turkey, swore oaths of friendship by drinking blood from cow's-horn cups with gold coins at the bottom.

Blood brothers

Bloodthirsty brotherhood rituals still survive today. In 2007, a gang in Italy was arrested. A newspaper reported that a new member would slice his veins and let out some blood into a bowl. The other members would mix the blood with water and everyone in the gang would drink it.

Ancient Greek myths are full of blood-loving monsters, but the only real-life blood-drinkers that we know about in ancient Greece were the wild women followers of the wine-god Dionysus, and priestesses called Oracles who were said to foretell the future.

How to be an Oracle

- Sit on a tall, three-legged (i.e. magic) stool, or hide mysteriously behind curtains.
- Breathe mind-bending fumes in caves deep underground.
- Chew poisonous leaves – they'll scramble your brain.
- On special occasions, drink blood.
- Utter weird, confused shrieks and mutterings.
- Priests will interpret your 'message from the gods' and pass it on to worshippers.

400–340 BC

Miss your family? Want extra power and prestige? Then drink up!

Early peoples hoped to win strenth and courage by drinking blood from slaughtered enemies or dead family members. Around 400 BC, horrified observers reported that 'each Scythian warrior drinks the blood of the first enemy he kills in battle', and that the Celts drink 'the blood of their dead ancestors, in order to gain their virtues'.

Around 340 BC, Roman citizens trembled at more wild rumours: an attacking army – the Samnites – wanted 'to drink our blood and tear our flesh'. Later Roman writers claimed that attacking Celts used enemy skulls as drinking-cups, and drank the blood of captured children.

Barbarians, they are – not civilised like us.

AD 40

Don't like someone, or feel threatened by them? Want an excuse to punish them? Accuse them of the worst things you can think of: drinking blood and/or killing babies!

From around AD 40, a new faith, Christianity, spread through Roman lands. Roman leaders distrusted Christians and said they were traitors. They claimed that Christians stole babies to eat at ghastly 'love feasts': 'Thirstily – oh horror! – they lick up the baby's blood; eagerly they divide its limbs.'

In fact, the red stuff the Christians drank at their ceremonies was wine. The Jews had religious laws which forbade them from drinking or eating blood; most early Christians had been brought up as Jews, so they followed the same rules. And those babies had been left outside to die by Roman families. The Christians were rescuing them!

Either those Roman leaders did not understand what the Christians were doing, or else they were deliberately trying to turn people against them.

AD 1144

This is tragic and terrible!

In AD 313, Emperor Constantine gave Christians freedom to worship throughout the Roman empire. They were no longer accused of drinking blood. Instead, for the next thousand years and more, Christians accused others of being blood-suckers. Their targets included heretics (religious dissidents) and people with incurable diseases (they thought sickness was a punishment sent by God). They also – horribly, wrongly and unjustly – accused the Jews. False accusations of this kind are known as 'blood libel'.

One of the first, and most damaging, examples of the blood libel against the Jews took place in the city of Norwich, England, in 1144. A young boy, William, disappeared, and was found dead a few days later. He had been brutally attacked, and his body was covered in wounds. Without any direct evidence, the citizens of Norwich blamed the Jews (a rich but persecuted minority) for the murder. William was made a saint, and Jewish people throughout Europe were soon being unjustly accused of murdering children, to drink their blood and use it in unholy rituals. Thousands of Jews were killed or injured in blood-libel riots and revenge attacks.

1450–1700

Beware, if you dabble in black magic...

Between around 1450 and 1700, there was a craze for hunting witches, first in Europe and then in North America. Religious disputes, economic crises and fast-changing communities all made people feel threatened and uneasy, so they sought outsiders, or people they feared, to take he blame. Thousands of innocent women – and some men – were accused of witchcraft, put on trial, found guilty and executed.

In *Malleus Maleficarum* (*Hammer of Witches*), a handbook for witch-hunters published in 1487, witches were said sometimes to disguise themselves as vampires. And, like vampires, they were accused of drinking blood.

For example, in 1692, a witness at a witch-trial at Salem, Massachusetts described what she believed to have been a real-life witches' meeting. There, two women offered her:

> some of their sweet bread and wine, and, she asking them what wine that was, one of them said it was blood and better than our wine.

The witness refused to eat or drink with the witches, and so they 'dreadfully afflicted her' (made her very ill) – or so she said.

Toil and trouble

Even Shakespeare mentions bloodthirsty witches in his plays. For example, in Hamlet (written in 1599–1600), Prince Hamlet says, at midnight, that he feels tempted to do evil:

'Tis now the very witching time of night,
When churchyards yawn and hell itself breathes out
Contagion[1] to this world; now could I drink hot blood
And do such bitter business as the day
Would quake to look on...

1. Contagion: disease.

157

1789

Running a revolution? Want to get rid of royalty?

In 1789, French people were hungry, powerless and very angry. They demanded a complete change in the way their country was governed, and fair shares of its wealth for all. They captured and killed rich, powerful nobles, including the French royal family. Before cutting off Queen Marie Antoinette's head, they called her 'blood-sucker of the French' and 'a monster'.

In real life, Marie Antoinette was a mild-mannered, rather silly woman. Her accusers knew that she did not drink human blood – but they passionately believed that royal taxes sucked all the wealth from ordinary men and women, destroying their lives, like vampires.

1883-1892

Look: vampires have crossed the Atlantic and reached the USA!

The deadly disease 'consumption' (now known as tuberculosis, or 'TB' for short) reached epidemic levels in the 19th century. TB was terrifying; no-one knew what caused it and there was no cure. It was also very infectious, especially in crowded homes, schools and workplaces. All too often, when one person caught TB, they passed it on to workmates, classroom friends and members of their own family. Sometimes, this led to terrible fears and suspicions...

Mercy! Mercy!

The Brown family lived in Rhode Island, USA. In 1883, Mary Brown died of TB. In 1884, her older daughter was killed by the same disease, then, in 1888, her son Edwin and her younger daughter Mercy also fell ill. Mercy died in 1892, and Edwin grew weaker, day by day.

Grieving and fearful, surviving members of the Brown family began to suspect that they were being attacked by something very sinister –

maybe even by a vampire. There was only one way to find out: they would dig up all the corpses and inspect them.

Mary Brown's body was just a skeleton. So was her older daughter's. But little Mercy's body was twisted in its grave – and was undecayed, and full of blood. Yes! She was a vampire, or so they said.[1] Yes, they must destroy her! They cut out Mercy's heart and burned it – and gave some of the ashes, as medicine, to poor, suffering Edwin. He died soon after.

1823

Here's some more ghastly medicine!

The ancient Romans thought that criminals' blood had the power to cure epilepsy. Amazingly, this belief lasted for over 2,000 years. In 1823, Danish storyteller Hans Christian Andersen saw parents make their sick son drink a cup of blood from an executed criminal, in a bid to cure him. And in many countries, crowds of women went to public beheadings – not to watch, but to dip their handkerchiefs in the blood, to use later for magic healing.

1. We know better, don't we? See pages 43–44.

Blood lust

For many centuries, sick, disturbed – or wicked – people have enjoyed killing for blood. Like Italian murderer Vincenzo Verzeni, convicted of sucking blood from six victims in 1872, they found that blood-drinking gave them 'immense satisfaction'. Many killed more than once; some also preyed on women and children. Most seem to have found pleasure in making other people suffer.

All their crimes were repulsive, but some were also mysterious, and others were simply weird. For example, in 1897, Jospeh Bacher toured France on a walking – and blood-sucking – holiday. He left behind a trail of at least 12 murdered victims, each with bite-wounds in the neck. In 1920, Baron von Sternberg-Ungarn was executed in Russia. He claimed to be a descendant of 13th-century Mongol conqueror Genghis Khan – and, like the Mongols, drank blood.

Some killers claimed to hear voices urging them to suck blood. Others say they killed because they believed that drinking blood was good for them, or they needed fresh blood to survive. In the USA, murderer Richard Chase killed animals for their blood, as well as people. When sentenced to death, he killed himself (in 1980), rather than face execution.

These murderers were mad or bad – and dangerous – but they were humans, not vampires. However, after the Dracula story became popular in the 20th century, men and women guilty of appalling crimes were regularly labelled 'vampire killers'. They were not vampires, of course, but a few tried to use vampirism as an excuse for their actions. In 2009, an American man threatened to torture to death the judge who was trying him. The man claimed to be the leader of a group called 'Vampyre Nation'.

Some murderers claimed that vampires had commanded them to kill, in return for the promise of everlasting life. Others revealed that they belonged to vampire cults – groups of people who dressed up as vampires, filing their teeth into fangs and drinking willing victims' blood. In 1996, this fantasy ran tragically out of control when a group of self-styled vampires murdered an elderly couple in the USA.

And, sad to report, in some places, ancient – and murderous – traditional blood-drinking customs still continued. In 2010, eyewitnesses claimed to have seen ritual killings of children in Uganda. It was said that blood and body parts were brought to secret places where it was believed that spirits would feed on them.

The Glasgow vampire

What's undead, has steel teeth, maybe wears a kilt, and lurks in Scotland's biggest city? Yes, you've guessed – it's the Glasgow vampire! Rumours of this killer creature flew round the city in the early 1950s. They led to crowds of excited, out-of-control children – over 300 at a time – gathering in a south Glasgow graveyard, all eager to see and attack the monster.

Where did these crowd-pulling rumours come from? At first, the police were puzzled. But then they found that the children had been reading some rather nasty American horror-comics. Law-makers were so worried by the threat of future disturbances that they banned the comics from being imported into Britain.

Now it's time to look at some very different natural-born killers. All kinds of creepy-crawlies (and one bat) drink blood – mostly from humans!

Never mind him. It's **me** you need to worry about!

Anopheles mosquito

164

Chapter Ten

It's only natural

eeling itchy? Skin bumpy and blotchy? Can't sleep or stop scratching? Clearly, you've been bitten! But by what kind of creature – and how might it harm you?

Natural-born blood-suckers

Places where humans and animals live are usually surrounded by many different kinds of insects. The main biters are various kinds of flies, lice, and fleas. Biting insects don't *look* dangerous. Nor do their fellow-predators, ticks, which belong to the spider family. Most are fragile and nearly weightless. Some are almost too small to see. Unlike storybook vampires, they won't drain you of vast quantities of blood. Yet many can kill you!

How do they do this? Mostly by injecting you with bacteria or parasites that cause disease. This way, they spread malaria, sleeping sickness, typhus, cholera, dysentery, deadly food poisoning – and many more maladies! Once inside your blood, these microscopic organisms multiply, spreading sickness right through your body.

It's usually only females that bite; they need a meal of protein from your blood to nourish them before they lay eggs which will hatch to become the next generation of biters. Each species has its own special kind of mouthpart. Most are sharp, to puncture the skin, and hollow, to suck up blood. Some are designed to spit saliva or other body fluids into a victim (you!) to help the biter digest its meal. Your body's reaction to these digestive juices is one of the main reasons why insect bites are so itchy.

WARNING
KEEP COVERED! SHOO HER AWAY!
SHE'S THE WORLD'S No. 1 KILLER

MOSQUITO!

Lurks in warm wet places all round the globe!

Fragile but fearsome!

☞ Spreads DEADLY malaria! ☜

500 MILLION victims every year –

– and 2 MILLION FATALITIES!

Lord Carnarvon, who helped discover the famous tomb of Egyptian pharaoh Tutankhamun, died from an infected mosquito bite in 1923. Some claimed the tomb was cursed...

Five Filthy Facts about Flies and Fleas, etc...

1. Horse-flies feed on the rotting remains of animals and vegetables. Manure and sewage are favourites, too. They inject little bits of all these into your blood when they bite you.

2. Female ticks have special elastic skin. As they feed, they swell to many times their normal size. They can survive, swollen, all winter. Why don't they burst? It's a mystery!

3. Fleas can jump 40 times their own height. And, when they've finished feeding, they scatter pellets of infected blood behind them. As well as spreading extremely dangerous bacteria as they bite, some fleas also spread tapeworms. These fasten themselves to animal intestines and suck food, growing all the time. They can reach 30 metres, or longer.

Rat fleas helped spread the world's most deadly outbreak of disease – the Black Death (bubonic plague) – around AD 1350. Then, one out of every three people died in many parts of Europe, North Africa and Asia.

4. Lice can't survive for more than two days without drinking blood. Head lice like clean hair, but body lice love dirty surroundings.

Tragic teenage heroine Anne Frank, who hid from the Nazis in World War Two and wrote a secret diary, died from typhus spread by body lice in a Nazi prison camp.

5. Bedbugs – these blood-sucking parasites don't just stay in the bedroom. They're spreading round the world – fast! – in travellers' clothes and luggage. They're armed with a sharp, barbed spike to pierce your skin and drink your blood. And they smell sweet, musty and horrible!

Now for one of my favourite transformations! I love to swoop around at night, in search of fresh victims...

Featherless birds? Mice with wings? Fabulous flyers with superhuman hearing – or nasty, dangerous monsters? There are over 900 different kinds of bats in the world, and they have a bad reputation which they don't deserve. They are said to 'haunt' ghostly ruins or spooky caves, or to fly with witches and wizards. In fact, most bats are completely harmless – they eat insects or fruit – but one bat *is* a blood-sucker. Its scientific name is *Desmodus rotundus*, but of course, it's been nicknamed 'vampire'.

In spite of its name, the vampire bat is nothing like the monster portrayed in Bram Stoker's book *Dracula*. There, the bat was massive and menacing. In real life, vampire bats are tiny – and shy.

Vampire bat basics

Body length: 5 cm
Wingspan: 20 cm
Weight: 25 g
Homeland: Central and South America
Family life: Lives in 'colonies' of 100–2,000
Flies: At night
Food: Blood from large mammals

Bat attack!

You're a vampire bat – and you're hungry! You need about 2 tablespoons of blood a day; how do you find your next meal?

- Use echo-location, sound and smell to find a suitable animal. Cows, pigs and horses are best, but you don't mind the occasional human.

- Land on its back, then use special heat-sensors on your nose to find blood capillaries (tiny channels) that run close under its skin.

- Use your canine teeth (the ones that look like fangs) to clip away a patch of its hair.

- Now the bare skin's exposed, use different teeth – your incisors (front ones) – to nibble a small hole in it. Your saliva will dribble down, but never mind! It contains a special chemical to mix with the animal's blood to stop it clotting and make it flow freely.

Vampire bat walking

- Just like a cat, you have a long tongue that can lap up liquids very quickly. Stick it into the hole you have made. The hollow groove down its middle will channel blood to the back of your throat, ready to swallow.

- You'll find a meal might take 20 minutes to complete. All that time, your digestive system will be very, very busy. It only absorbs nourishment from the red cells (see page 16) in the blood – and begins to excrete (push out) the leftovers as faeces and urine while you are still feeding!

A bat's best friend...

...is another bat! Because vampire bats are so small, they cannot store much energy from their food. Unless they eat every two or three days, they will die. So, if a bat becomes too weak and hungry to fly, other members of its colony will regurgitate (sick up) the remains of their last meals to feed it!

Bet you didn't know we could do this!

Vampires and werewolves

It's full moon, and midnight. What's that gliding grey among the trees? Is it man or beast?

In Bram Stoker's novel, Dracula has the power of shape-shifting. He can transform himself into a wolf, a giant bat and several other sinister apparitions. He can also command the howling wolves that threaten travellers venturing towards his castle – and the ravenous wolf-pack that devours the poor peasant woman who begs him to return her stolen baby. He even speaks fondly of these bloodthirsty beasts, calling them 'the children of the night'. And – remember! – he has claw-like nails and very hairy hands.

Dracula's ability to change shape, and his kinship with killer creatures, is not only magical. It also shows very clearly that he has strong links with savage natural forces. These are less than human – and beyond human control. Many vampire myths suggest the same close connection between wolves and vampires. The name *upir* itself (see page 45) comes from a word that can also mean 'werewolf'.

What do these myths mean? What are they trying to tell us? Probably that fierce, selfish desires lie deep inside every human. If they are not controlled, by religion, or tradition, or a 'civilised' education, they have terrible powers to harm other people – and destroy us.

Shock horror!

Vampires in modern media

he dark, bloodstained tale of Dracula, the world's most famous vampire, was not a best-seller at the time it first appeared. Yet today, vampires are some of the most popular media characters. They appear in all kinds of entertainments, from Hollywood epics to manga comics, and from TV serials to fantasy games, blogs and webrings. Over 200 films have been made featuring Dracula himself – after Sherlock Holmes, he's the literary character who's been filmed most often.

There have been vampire musicals (including the cult *Rocky Horror Show*, 1973, filmed in 1975 as *The Rocky Horror Picture Show*) and vampire classical ballets. Countless bands have sung about vampires, or dressed like them. Vampires have inspired TV cartoons such as *Count Duckula* (UK, 1988–1993), and puppet shows. *Sesame Street*'s mathematical Transylvanian 'Count von Count' first appeared on American screens in 1972. There is even 'Count Chocula', a chocolate-flavoured children's breakfast cereal, created (if that's the word) in 1971 and still on sale in the USA.

Dangerous games

Influenced by modern media, some would-be 'living vampires' wear flapping black cloaks and deathly-pale make-up and have their teeth filed into fangs. They meet to study vampire lore, or to act out role-playing games based on chilling stories. A strange – and illegal – few claim to hold real-life vampire parties, where they drink willing victims' blood.

**Don't try this, even for a joke or a dare.
You could die from an incurable disease.**

Moving pictures

The earliest-known vampire film was created in 1896, a year before Bram Stoker completed his famous novel, *Dracula*. Called *The Haunted Castle*, and just 50 seconds long, it featured a scary, scape-shifting 'undead' figure (first a skeleton, then a warrior knight in armour) that could never be destroyed. (It also featured a comic chair that did not want to be sat upon – but that is another story.) The film's director, French inventor Georges Méliès, was one of the great pioneers of cinema. His experimental 'moving pictures' helped create the 20th century's most influential media: films and TV. And they made vampires popular.

Would you believe it? The next batch of vampire films ignored me completely. They were all about women!

'Vamps'

From around 1909 to 1920, many vampire films were based on a shocking poem by one of Britain's most popular writers, Rudyard Kipling. Written in 1897 (the year that *Dracula* was published), and called 'The Vampire', it described how a foolish man was destroyed by a female monster. To him, she appeared as 'his lady fair', but underneath, she was nothing more than 'a rag and a bone and a hank of hair', who did not – and could not – care about the men who fell hopelessly in love with her.

Kipling's misogynistic poem inspired many early silent films, such as *The Vampire*, made in 1913, and *A Fool There Was*, two years later. They all featured 'vamps' (short for 'vampiresses'): young, glamorous, heartless women played by top stars. The most famous was dark-eyed, scantily clad Theda Bara, from the USA.

> 'The reason good women like me and flock to my pictures is that there is a little bit of vampire instinct in every woman.'
>
> Theda Bara (1885–1955)

At last, a film about me – and they had it banned!

Nosferatu

In 1922, German director Friedrich Murnau made a truly terrifying film, *Nosferatu* ('Bird of Death'), featuring a monstrous male vampire. The film's plot was so closely based on Bram Stoker's book that Stoker's family protested. (In Britain at that time, a book could not be copied for 50 years after the death of its author.) British law-courts ordered that all copies of *Nosferatu* should be destroyed. Most were, but a few tattered prints survived. In 1994 their remains were pieced together, and *Nosferatu* was shown again. It's a scary masterpiece!

Aha! Now it gets better. Here comes my big entrance!

Make sure the camera shows my best side.

A lasting image

Bram Stoker's book *Dracula* was not protected by copyright law in the USA – and American playwrights and film-makers recognised a good horror story when they saw one! So, in 1927, a thrilling stage version of *Dracula* was performed on Broadway (the home of top theatres in New York). The part of Dracula was played by tall, dark, sinisterly handsome Béla Lugosi, a Hungarian actor who had been born in Transylvania, just like Dracula himself. The play was a great success, and Lugosi was excellent as the vampire villain. He made Dracula seem real and believable – and therefore all the more horrifying! In 1931, Lugosi starred in the first Hollywood film version of *Dracula*, creating the image of the deathly-pale, black-cloaked, menacing vampire that has lasted until today.

Many later vampire films were inspired by Lugosi's performance – and their plots featured similar scenes of haunting and blood-sucking. Christopher Lee starred in some of the most successful. But other film-makers used the idea and image of vampires in an astonishing variety of ways – from monster comedies, for example *Abbott and Costello Meet Frankenstein* (1948), through fantasies about vampire females, such as *Blood and Roses* (1960), to modern-day vampires with attitude, especially *Blacula* (starring an African-American cast, 1975) and epics that mingled vampire lore with science fiction, most famously in *The Last Man on Earth* (1964). The Dracula family of vampires expanded, as well, from *Daughter of Dracula* (1936) to *Dracula and Son* (1976) and even (in 1978) *Dracula's Dog*!

A new kind of vampire

Writers of books were not going to be left behind in this vampire bonanza. Blood-sucking monsters featured in many novels of the late 20th century, and this fashion has remained popular into the new millennium. Modern vampire tales for adults range from classic horror fiction, such as *Salem's Lot* (1975) by Stephen King, to supernatural detective stories, like the Southern Vampire Mysteries (since 2001) by Charlaine Harris. There are also vampire romances, vampire historical novels, vampire science fiction, vampire voodoo tales and vampire pornography. Some vampire novels have been made into feature films; many more have inspired popular drama series on TV. The TV series *Buffy the Vampire Slayer* (1997–2003) attracted a huge following.

Multi-volume series of vampire stories sell millions of copies right round the world. The most famous of these are the Barnabas Collins books (1966–1971) by Marilyn Ross, the Vampire Chronicles (1996–2003) by Anne Rice, and the Twilight saga (2005–2008) by Stephenie Meyer. But there are many, many others – including one series written especially for young adults, by Darren Shan. Starting with *Cirque du Freak* (2000), it features a boy learning to be – no, not a cunning wizard, but a dangerous vampire.

Many modern stories feature an entirely new kind of vampire: a dangerously handsome hero who, unlike Dracula and earlier east-European predators, does not want to do harm. In some series, the vampire is a trapped, tragic, tormented figure. In some, he belongs to a 'normal' community, and leads a life of family quarrels and neighbourhood dramas, just like in 'soaps' on TV. In others, the vampire is a seductive, compelling, male romantic hero – with fangs.

The women and children in these stories also include a wide range of characters – from spooky child vampires and strong, clever female vampire-hunters to a famously pure (but secretly tempted) vampire girlfriend. Will she, or won't she, get bitten…?

…and if she does, then what, oh what, happens afterwards? I really want to know! And that, dear reader, is why so many of us still love to read vampire stories.

It doesn't matter that classic vampires like me don't exist, or that modern writers have invented 'vampires' that look, speak, feed and behave completely differently from us old-style blood-suckers. Most people are still fascinated by any creature with superhuman strength and magic powers, who can live for ever. The dreadful price of vampire eternal life – the death and suffering of others – is far too high, of course. But sometimes, in a well-told tale, it can seem very tempting. In the epic struggle between good and evil, victims and vampires, we all get involved – and we all want to know who's going to win!

Glossary

Afterlife According to many religions, the life of the soul which continues after the death of the body.

artery A blood vessel that carries oxygen-rich blood from the lungs towards other parts of the body.

bacteria Microscopic organisms, some of which can cause disease.

canine teeth The narrow, pointed teeth immediately behind the front teeth in humans and many other mammals.

capillaries The smallest blood vessels in the body.

circulation The movement of blood around the body, pumped by the heart.

exorcism A religious rite intended to expel evil spirits.

haemoglobin The protein that makes blood red.

incisors Front teeth.

pagan Following a religion other than Christianity, Judaism or Islam.

parasite A living organism that lives and feeds on another living organism.

plasma The liquid part of blood.

platelets Cells that help blood to clot.

transfusion A medical procedure for transferring blood from one living body to another.

undead, the In folklore, creatures that are dead, but able to behave as though still alive.

vein A blood vessel that carries stale blood back towards the lungs to receive more oxygen.

zombie According to Voodoo belief, a dead body which can move like a living person but has no mind of its own.

Timeline of vampire history

before 2000 BC Myths from Egypt, Babylon, India, China and elsewhere feature deadly, blood-sucking, supernatural creatures.

c.800 BC Greek poet Homer describes blood-drinking, undead ghosts.

c.600–100 BC Blood-drinking monsters are portrayed in Greek myths, legends and works of art.

c.500 BC Greek travellers report blood-drinking rituals among the Scythian peoples of Central Asia.

c.300 BC – AD 300 Roman myths tell of vampire-like monsters such as the blood-drinking strix.

c.100 BC – AD 100 Roman soldiers describe blood-drinking among their enemies, especially the Celts.

c.AD 100 Romans accuse early Christians of drinking babies' blood. Roman crowds drink gladiators' blood, to bring them strength and power. Some Romans believe that criminals' blood can cure mental illness.

c.200–1000 Christian leaders teach that people who live wicked lives will be punished after death. Many Christians believe that the ghosts of the dead can return to harm the living.

c.1000 Christians in eastern Europe believe the bodies of wicked people will not decay, but can be brought back to life by the devil or by their own unquiet spirits.

1047 First-known written reference to a vampire (*upir likhiy*), in Russia.

c.1100–1500 'Blood libel': Jewish people unjustly accused of drinking children's blood.

c.1190 Monk William of Newburgh reports a vampire ghost in England.

c.1200 Scandinavian writer Saxo Grammaticus records a story of Viking vampires.

1431–1476 Reign of Vlad III, cruel ruler of Wallachia (now part of Romania). He is known as Vlad 'Dracula' (= Son of the Dragon, or Son of the Devil).

c.1450–1700 Witch-hunting panic in Europe and, after 1600, in European colonies in America.

1484 *Malleus Maleficarum* (*Hammer of Witches*), a guide to witch-hunting, is published in Germany. It accuses witches of drinking blood.

1560–1614 Life of probable mass-murderer Elizabeth Báthory, wrongly called 'the female Dracula'.

c.1600–1800 'Vampire panics' in eastern Europe.

1628 English scientist William Harvey discovers the double circulation of the blood (from lungs to heart, and from heart to limbs).

1734 First recorded (written) use of the word 'vampire' in English.

1746 French monk Dom Augustin Calmet publishes his collection of vampire folklore and superstitions.

1748 Heinrich August Ossenfelder writes the first 'literary' vampire poem, in Austria.

1749 French scientist the Comte de Buffon publishes the first volume of his *Natural History*. He is the first to call blood-sucking bats 'vampire bats'.

1755 Empress Maria Theresa of Austria-Hungary sends scientists to investigate vampire panics.

1819 English doctor John Polidori writes shocking short story, *The Vampyre*. His villain is inspired by celebrity poet, Lord Byron.

1845–1847 *Varney the Vampire* appears in instalments. The villain is one of the first sympathetic vampires, who hates being a killer but is powerless to change.

Timeline of vampire history

1872 *Carmilla*, by Irish writer Sheridan Le Fanu, features a female vampire who preys on girls.

1890s Vampire panic as TB spreads through New England. Mercy Brown's body is dug up and destroyed.

1894–1897 Irish novelist Bram Stoker writes *Dracula*.

1896 Georges Méliès directs the first-ever vampire moving picture.

1922 Horror movie *Nosferatu*, based on the novel *Dracula*. It is banned after complaints from Bram Stoker's family.

1931 Hungarian actor Béla Lugosi stars in Hollywood film *Dracula*, creating modern classic vampire image.

1958 Christopher Lee portrays a handsome, seductive vampire in *Horror of Dracula* and many later films.

1975 Stephen King publishes his classic vampire story, *Salem's Lot*.

1992 'Vampire killer' Andrei Chikatilo, of Russia, confesses to killing 55 people and drinking their blood.

1992 *Bram Stoker's Dracula*, starring Gary Oldman, is praised for faithfully following Stoker's original story.

1994 Tom Cruise and Brad Pitt star in romantic Hollywood film *Interview with the Vampire*.

1992 Feature film *Buffy the Vampire-Slayer*, which later gives rise to a long-running TV series (1997–2003).

1996 Anne Rice publishes the first of her Vampire Chronicles, featuring a tragic, romantic vampire.

2005 Stephenie Meyer's Twilight series features an American teenage girl and her vampire boyfriend.

2009 Charlaine Harris's Southern Vampire Mysteries series is adapted for US TV.

2010 Director Tim Burton plans to film Seth Grahame-Smith's novel *Abraham Lincoln, Vampire Hunter*.

Index

Index

Other titles in The Cherished Library

Ancient Egypt
A Very Peculiar History
The Art of Embalming:
Mummy Myth and Magic
With added Squishy Bits
Jim Pipe
ISBN: 978-1-906714-92-5

Brighton
A Very Peculiar History
With added Hove, actually
David Arscott
ISBN: 978-1-906714-89-5

Ireland
A Very Peculiar History
With NO added Blarney
Jim Pipe
ISBN: 978-1-905638-98-7

Rations
A Very Peculiar History
With NO added Butter
David Arscott
ISBN: 978-1-907184-25-3

London
A Very Peculiar History
With added Jellied Eels
Jim Pipe
ISBN: 978-1-907184-26-0

Heroes, Gods and Monsters of
Ancient Greek Mythology
Michael Ford
ISBN: 978-1-906370-92-3

Scotland
A Very Peculiar History
With NO added Haggis
or Bagpipes
**Vol. 1: From ancient times
to Robert the Bruce**
ISBN: 978-1-906370-91-6

**Vol. 2: From the Stewarts
to modern Scotland**
ISBN: 978-1-906714-79-6

Fiona Macdonald

The Blitz
A Very Peculiar History
With NO added Doodlebugs
David Arscott
ISBN: 978-1-907184-18-5

Wales
A Very Peculiar History
With NO added Laverbread
Rupert Matthews
ISBN: 978-1-907184-19-2

The World Cup
A Very Peculiar History
With NO added Time
David Arscott
ISBN: 978-1-907184-38-3

Heroes, Gods and Monsters of
Celtic Mythology
Fiona Macdonald
ISBN: 978-1-905638-97-0